PERSONAL MASTERY

A Leader's Guide to Finding Meaning and Fulfillment in the Modern World

Jung Wing Wan, PhD

Foreword by Tomas Svitorka

**Personal Mastery
A Leader's Guide to Finding Meaning and Fulfillment
In The Modern World**
© 2025 Jung Wing Wan

All rights reserved. No part of this book may be reproduced, stored in a retrieval system or transmitted in any form or by any means (electronic, mechanical, photocopy, recording, scanning or other) except for brief quotations in critical reviews or articles, without the prior written permission of the publisher.

ISBN: 9781068426209 Paperback

Published by: Inspired By Publishing

The strategies in this book are presented primarily for enjoyment and educational purposes. Every effort has been made to trace copyright holders and obtain their permission for the use of copyright material.

The information and resources provided in this book are based upon the authors' personal experiences. Any outcome, income statements or other results, are based on the authors' experiences and there is no guarantee that your experience will be the same. There is an inherent risk in any business enterprise or activity and there is no guarantee that you will have similar results as the author as a result of reading this book.

The author reserves the right to make changes and assumes no responsibility or liability whatsoever on behalf of any purchaser or reader of these materials.

Dedication

This book is dedicated to:
Mum and Dad;
my wonderful children, Daniel and Emily,
who make us proud;
my dear, loving wife Yen Ming;
and God, who makes all things possible.

Foreword

There's no shortage of advice on personal development. Everywhere you turn, someone is offering insights or quick fixes for growth. But real progress – the kind that lasts and fulfils – requires more: depth, authenticity and practicality. That's what makes *Personal Mastery* so powerful. It's not just another book of ideas; it's a framework for action and fulfilling growth.

Through my many years of coaching ambitious professionals and entrepreneurs, I've seen countless approaches to personal and professional transformation. What I love about Jung's approach is how it takes you beyond surface-level solutions. It challenges readers to reflect on who they are, their mindset and the direction of their growth, guiding them to create meaningful change. This book reminds us that mastery isn't a destination but a practice – a way of living intentionally and authentically.

Jung Wing Wan, PhD, embodies this mindset. I first met him in 2022 when he made the bold decision to transition from a successful corporate career to coaching – a path he approached not as another career but as a calling. Throughout our work together, I saw his commitment to learning and mastering the principles he shares in this book. Jung's unique combination of discipline, empathy and an unwavering commitment to excellence is reflected on every page.

Jung's book is full of deep insights and practical tips. While he shares his own experiences, the real value lies in how universally applicable the lessons are. He doesn't just tell you what to do – he equips you with the right tools, ideas and questions so that you can reflect, act and grow.

There are two reasons this book is such an important contribution.

First, it provides a guide to deep transformation. It's one thing to grasp concepts like self-awareness or purpose; it's another thing to understand how to truly embody and live them. This book helps you do that.

Second, it explores the nature of success. Today, success isn't just about traditional milestones like financial security – it's about balance, fulfilment and making a meaningful impact. Jung's book speaks directly to these values.

Foreword

If you're holding this book, it's likely because you're ready to take the next step in your journey. My advice? Approach it with curiosity and a willingness to deeply explore who you are. Don't look for a formula or a checklist. This is an invitation to reflect, explore and evolve.

In the crowded space of personal development, *Personal Mastery* stands out. It's sincere, substantive and grounded in real experience. It invites you to go beyond surface-level change and approach growth as a lifelong commitment to yourself.

Jung has created something of true value here – a guide that challenges, inspires and equips you to raise your standards and pursue mastery with clarity and purpose.

Enjoy the journey.

Tomas Svitorka
Life & Performance Coach,
Speaker, Entrepreneur

Contents

Introduction	1
Section 1 - Taking Back Control	**7**
Chapter 1 - Self Awareness	9
Chapter 2 - Self Knowledge	31
Chapter 3 - Self Management	45
Section 2 - Starting to Lead	**81**
Chapter 4 - Self Motivation	83
Chapter 5 - Resilience	95
Chapter 6 - Self Confidence	109
Section 3 - Winning More	**121**
Chapter 7 - Realistic Optimism	123
Chapter 8 - Growth Mindset	133
Chapter 9 - Decision-Making	147

Section 4 - Finding Purpose   **161**

Chapter 10 - Purpose   163

Conclusion   187

Epilogue   195

Resources   196

References   197

Acknowlegements   200

About the Author   202

Introduction

This book *Personal Mastery: A Leader's Guide to Finding Meaning and Fulfilment in the Modern World* is for you if you want to know how to become more effective, happy and successful, both at work and in your personal life. You may already be accomplished in your career or feel that what you do is just not enough. Perhaps feelings of stress, frustration, irritation and being lost without direction are frequent features of your daily experience.

I will take you on a journey into the unknown – the unknown being what more you are capable of, a discovery made by going within yourself. By adopting a detached and curious mindset without self-judgement, you can expect to find surprises and personal truths that you already know about but are yet to appreciate. Has anyone ever told you how much something you said or did made them feel good?

In writing this book – intentionally handwritten with my trusty fountain pen – I do not in any way claim to be a teacher, master or guru. I do, however, write as a dutiful student keen to share perspectives and insights as your guide, one who is on his own life journey of self-discovery just as you may be, a fellow human being living on this planet we call home.

As a coach, I challenge your current understanding, beliefs and perceptions of reality to help you grow to be a more fulfilled, empowered and whole human being.

Why is this important? Simply put, it is because if we can all discover our own unique combination of talents and skills and learn to use them fully, we can do so much more to help ourselves and others, making the world we live in a better place. This is where we can all find purpose and meaning.

Prior to becoming a coach, I had a 25-year corporate career in the pharmaceutical industry, which took me to more than 30 countries. I practise the Chinese martial arts of Taichi and Xing Yi, which have helped me develop a mindset of personal mastery – the practice of becoming a better version of oneself. I am an avid callisthenics athlete and a runner. I also love the art of Chinese cooking and BBQs. My earlier academic path included a PhD in Chemistry and a year in France as an exchange student. I love learning languages and speak Chinese (Cantonese and Mandarin), French, and Spanish, and, as of writing, I am learning Korean. I have been married now for 24 years with two wonderful children. I also serve as a leader and elder at a church in central London.

I'll be introducing my method called the Jung Personal Mastery Method. This method consists of 10 core pillars, which I use to help my clients develop their own ability to lead in life and work.

Introduction

I originally developed this method to help me in my journey towards becoming a better coach for the people I help, as well as to become better as a leader of my self.

Jung Personal Mastery Method

This book is split into four main sections, within which I'll introduce you to the 10 pillars.

Section 1: Take Back Control

To make a difference in the way you live and work in the world, it is important to start by regaining your ability to control what you can, giving you a good place to begin changing. It starts with self-awareness, continues with developing self-knowledge and then ends with self-management.

Section 2: Starting to Lead

Changing your life requires personal development through good self-motivation coupled with resilience to handle stress and change, and trust in your abilities (self-confidence).

Section 3: Winning More

The way to more effective self-leadership includes adopting a better mindset that empowers you sustainably. This includes realising that you have the freedom to act in any situation (realistic optimism), the freedom to keep learning and growing (growth mindset), and, lastly, the freedom to make your own decisions (decision-making).

Section 4: Finding Purpose

To be an efficient and effective leader, you must have more than just the ability to apply leadership skills. You must also have a sense of direction and meaning. By being connected to your purpose, you will lead even more authentically and lead others with you.

Introduction

My aim is that by sharing the insights and actionable tips I have collected and developed, I can help make your experience both at work and in your personal life that little brighter and, more importantly, grounded in practical possibility. As you read this book, expect to be challenged in your experiences, perspectives and understanding. I recommend that you take your time and go through this book deliberately. Personal growth, which involves gaining a better understanding of ourselves, is not a race from start to finish but a journey to be savoured and experienced. Insights gained develop when allowed time to mature – rather like a fine wine.

> *"We were born with wings, but never taught to fly."*
> – "Glass" by Kasabian

I hope that this book helps you to flex those metaphorical wings that are uniquely yours and start flying! There are people who need you to get going!

Section 1
Taking Back Control

*"Measurement is the first step that leads to control and eventually to improvement.
If you can't measure something, you can't understand it.
If you can't understand it, you can't control it.
If you can't control it, you can't improve it."*

– H. James Harrington

Chapter 1
Self Awareness
"Looking Into the Mirror"

"Until you make the unconscious conscious, it will direct your life and you will call it fate."

– Carl Jung

The Self-Awareness Pillar of Personal Mastery

Where do we start? "At the beginning" is the rhetorical answer! In order to begin taking back control of your life and work on your journey of self development, the starting place is with awareness – self awareness. In this chapter, we start with an exploration of what self awareness is, what makes it important and how to practise it for your own personal growth.

A Personal Journey of Self Awareness

I didn't know what was wrong with me. I was keen to do my best at work and in my studies. I was punctual. I had an impeccable attendance record throughout my education and career. I was always learning new techniques and skills. I appeared to be doing all the right things. So what was wrong? Was anything wrong? What was I missing? Was anything missing?

This was not the sort of problem I could go to ask someone for their professional opinion. I certainly did not think it to be an issue to trouble my family doctor with. I imagined she'd say, "Relax, take breaks…" – nothing I'd feel had any real impact to resolve my issue. But who could I talk to about my problem? Come to think of it, was there even a problem? Should I just let it go and keep living my life, doing what I was doing, or indeed "meant to be doing"?

Maybe that's where the problem was coming from! What was I meant to be doing?! I really did not know. I had grown up as a diligent individual, living with an attitude of filial piety towards my Hong Kong Chinese immigrant parents, never losing sight of my study and work obligations. I grew up as the eldest of four children; as the oldest and a son, I assumed the top responsibility of being a role model. It became part of who I was. I studied hard and always handed in my assignments on time. I showed up with enthusiasm, was diligent in my work and did everything that could be expected of me – yet despite being told I was doing a "good job," I found myself often overlooked when work opportunities came up. It was a repeated source of frustration and anxiety, but no one knew about my inner turmoil. No one knew or understood what I was experiencing. Somehow, I did a good job of keeping it all hidden.

I started my career in the pharmaceutical industry with a postgraduate PhD degree. I thought of myself as relatively self-aware, as someone who lived to high standards, morally and ethically. However, over time, I realised that many people I met and worked with did not understand me well. I later learned that self awareness is not something we do once and forget, it is something to work on continually for self improvement. Often, it can improve significantly, that is, if one asks for help.

So what is self awareness? And what makes it so important, especially if we want to become better versions of ourselves, for our self improvement?

If I were to illustrate what self awareness is with one word, I'd say that word is "Awakening."

I am not suggesting that you and I are asleep in life. When you are asleep, you are unconscious and unaware of what is happening around you – until something triggers you to wake up. When you wake up, you become aware of yourself, where you are, the time, and your feelings, and you realise that you need to get up to start your day. There are things we do without a second thought, almost as if we are doing them on autopilot, so to speak. A lot of these actions are done with good efficiency. However, what if we want or need to do something differently, perhaps to achieve a better result? What then?

Well, here we would need to be conscious – "more awake," if you like – of what we do unconsciously and automatically. We would need to "awaken" to what we have been doing automatically. I say "do" here, but it could equally apply to our feelings and emotions and the words we say (how we communicate).

As people go about their daily routines, whether at work or in their personal lives, we often do things automatically. This is a reflection of how our brains naturally like to operate. If we can do what we need to do without too much conscious thought, our brains can free up some cognitive bandwidth to pay attention to something else (or do nothing at all!).

Let us say you were to improve your tennis gameplay. You have two options for going about it:

Option A: You play tennis like before, without thinking or analysing your current ability and performance and without feedback.

Option B: You recruit a tennis coach who gives you feedback on your current ability and performance and offers tips on how to improve.

By choosing option A, there could be some improvement, just because you play more and thereby get "practice."

With option B, you stand to make bigger gains as you would get updated and timely expert evaluations of your performance, plus informed tips on how to improve incrementally.

There is a strong probability that out of these two options, you would go for option B, as long as you hold a strong desire to improve your tennis game.

Let's go deeper.

On Option A: When you do something alone with the desire to improve, you rely on your own current level of awareness. You see what you want to see. In other words, your perception of your performance would likely be limited by your expectations, understanding and your habits of thought. It makes me think of what Albert Einstein is oft-misquoted for having said: "Insanity is doing the same thing over and over again and expecting different results." Another saying: "You can't solve a problem with the same mind that created it."

I find myself prone to overthinking. During these episodes, my thoughts tend to spiral, going round and round in circles, often into negative thoughts. Has this happened to you?

We need to do our work to develop and grow, whether it is a skill or ability. To apply an exercise analogy: "You have to put in the reps to get stronger muscles."

When I choose to rely on myself to develop a given skill, I have only my feedback and perspective.

Let's look at Option B again.

This time, you have someone who is observing you as you practice tennis – a coach. Your coach will give qualified feedback on how you are playing tennis. They will suggest what you can do to improve. The coach will point out what you are doing well. They will encourage you too, enabling you to keep playing and improving. In this scenario, the player (you) gets more enhanced self awareness of their ability to perform.

A Chinese saying goes, "The spectator sees more of the game than the players." When you are deep in the game, so to speak, you only see your bit of it. The spectator or coach has a completely different perspective of what is happening. The result is better self awareness, whether it is applied to a skill or task you do in daily life.

Self awareness as a concept is often illustrated by the act of gazing at ourselves in the mirror. By paying attention to ourselves to understand the person looking back at us, we can benefit by knowing how we are in the present time.

Self Awareness of Our Thoughts

When we are asked the question, "How are you?", how do we normally answer? Often, our responses are given in reflex, sounding like "I'm fine", "Not too bad," or "Great! How about you?" These responses are said without much thought or even awareness. I appreciate that there may be very practical reasons for not engaging in a conversation every time someone asks how you are, such as limited time or that you don't want to share anything too personal.

If you have a moment with yourself – when it is safe to do so (e.g. not driving or operating machinery) – asking yourself questions to answer as truthfully as possible can prove to be an interesting exercise or indeed a regular practice. How often do we stop and "check in" with ourselves on how we are? After all, we are more likely to ask others how they are! Socrates is famously quoted as saying, "The unexamined life is not worth living." Presumably, Socrates meant that our lives become more enriching and interesting when we look at ourselves in them.

The only way to develop self awareness is to practice it! Time to do a simple thought observation exercise. The following is a short activity involving the act of noticing the thoughts as they come to you and letting them go thereafter. It will help you improve the self awareness you have of your thoughts. You may find it insightful.

Thought Observation Exercise: The 5-Minute Thought Log

Objective: Increase awareness of habitual thought patterns.

Instructions: Set a timer for five minutes. Sit quietly and observe your thoughts as they arise without judgment. Write down the thoughts in real time as they come to you. After the timer ends, review your notes and categorise thoughts as positive, neutral or negative. Reflect on what you notice about recurring themes or triggers in your thought patterns.

Takeaway: Notice recurring themes or triggers for your thought patterns.

This exercise may be easy in principle and, at the same time, challenging to do – that is fine. Spending a couple of minutes in your day to notice your thoughts is a great start.

For me, what makes this exercise of noticing your thoughts so revealing is that you become an observer of your thoughts. You become like a detached witness to the thoughts that enter your mind.

By noticing your thoughts without engaging with them, you will develop your ability to understand them and how they influence what you feel, say and do. Marcus Aurelius, the well-known Stoic and Roman emperor, once wisely observed: "The happiness of your life depends on the quality of your thoughts."

What we notice about our thoughts is that they come unbidden, with a life of their own. Some are repeated thoughts. Some will seem odd. Some may be positive while others less so. These will likely be thoughts you may simply prefer to keep to yourself. While you may notice the quality of your thoughts, it is also important to exercise detachment from them (i.e. to observe without judgement).

You may start to realise how some thoughts are "triggered" by other thoughts, feelings or what you are experiencing or have experienced. If you have just watched a thought-provoking film or television programme, are you not more likely to be still thinking about it hours after you have watched it?

At this point, I recall a well-known poem taught to children in Chinese language-speaking schools called "Silent Night Thoughts" (靜夜思) [jìng yè sī] by the Tang dynasty poet Li Bai:

> "Before my bed lies a pool of moon bright,
> I could imagine that it's frost on the ground,
> I look up and see the bright shining moon,
> Bowing my head, I am thinking of home."

The poet talks of being away for long periods on study or duties and at the time of the Mid Autumn Festival (with the full harvest moon), he is struck with homesickness, thinking of home and family. Think of this festival for the Chinese as being like Christmas or Thanksgiving in the US when families traditionally gather to celebrate. You, as the reader, will observe how the sight of something – the moon, in this case – triggers the poet to think of something else (home and family). I love how this Tang poem, composed in the characteristic four lines of five Chinese characters, eloquently captures a poignant moment of self awareness.

To stay still just to notice your thoughts can prove to be challenging, especially if you are doing this as a novice. This practice is essentially an exercise of mindfulness and allows your mind to calm down and develop mental clarity. As the French philosopher Blaise Pascal famously observed, "All of humanity's ills stem from man's inability to sit quietly in a room alone."

I recall once noticing a young man at my local gym gazing more at his phone than doing his physical workout. The time he spent doing exercises was relatively small compared to his scrolling. After some swimming, I retired to the sauna and was shortly joined by the same young man. During the 10 minutes I was there, I focused on my breathing while keeping still with my eyes closed.

I could hear my fellow sauna user frequently brushing the sweat off his face, changing his seating position and sipping water from his water canister. I know that sitting still in a hot sauna can be uncomfortable, and this seemed to be very much the case for this young man. Or perhaps it was also because he was not within arms reach of his smartphone! Our modern-day smart devices are great tools, but they do an exceptional job of meeting our human need for constant stimulation by giving access to an ever-present source of distraction. I became more distracted by my thoughts of what this young man was doing, and so my mind was noticeably centred on him! Well, I did notice where my thoughts were going eventually! It does not take much to distract us from our train of thought.

It is to be expected that our thoughts will turn at the hint of distraction. Rather than berating ourselves for getting distracted (or worse, giving up), it is more helpful to acknowledge this (without self judgement) and return to observing our thoughts. The simple act of noticing ourselves when we get distracted is itself a thought, and so the key is not to run after that thought if you can, but simply to let it go.

The more we practise observing our thoughts, the better our ability to influence the nature of thoughts that come to us and the better our general state of mental well-being. Our thoughts influence our emotions, so we will next explore the self awareness of our emotions and what we can do about it.

Self Awareness of Our Emotions

You and I are human beings, individuals who experience emotions. I like how Tony Robbins describes emotions as "energy in motion," and he is spot on to point out that we as emotional beings are often driven by emotion!

How Aware Are You of Your Emotions in Daily Life?

I came across a retelling of a Zen parable from Daniel Goleman's book *Emotional Intelligence*[1] that can serve as an insightful illustration.

In the parable, a brusque samurai warrior approaches a Zen master who is deep in meditation. With a loud, discourteous voice, the warrior demanded from the master, "Tell me the nature of heaven and hell!" The master opened his eyes, glared into the warrior's eyes and scornfully replied, "Why should I waste my time to explain anything to an insolent fool like you!" On hearing this insult, the warrior flew into a rage, drew out his sword, poised to strike down the seated monk, saying, "I'll cut you down in an instant for that!" Looking coolly into the warrior's gaze, the monk calmly stated, "That's hell."

At this, the warrior froze and realised what had just happened. He understood that his anger had taken control of him to the point where he could easily have killed someone without further thought. He quickly sheathed his weapon, put it to one side, and bowed deeply with clasped hands, asking for forgiveness and compassion from the monk. He was grateful to the monk for this valuable insight. The Zen monk then smiled gently in acknowledgement, saying, "That's heaven."

I am not focusing on what you may already understand as "heaven" and "hell" but rather the valuable insights on emotional self awareness we get from this story.

One insight is how powerful and destructive emotions can be when we are unaware of how they affect our words (communication), actions (behaviour) and our thoughts. The warrior was trapped momentarily by his own "prison," one of fury, resentment, hatred and self righteousness.

Another is that with the simple act of becoming aware of our own emotional state, we can exert better control over how we feel next.

And thirdly, by arriving at a place of better understanding, we get to move forward into better outcomes.

Emotions can and have been labelled as either "good" or "bad." For example, anger is often called a "bad emotion" typically because we can all recall examples of people – including ourselves – who were gripped by anger, outwardly or inwardly. When in anger, we may say or do things we later regret. What makes anger appear negative is the way we often feel with it in play. It is powerful and consumes a lot of energy, even when we manage to contain it inside (and keeping it in is not a healthy practice either – more on that later). However, anger, on the other hand, can be a positively powerful emotion. If an intruder is trespassing into your home, then the emotion of anger helps you to be fully alert and take action (I hope by appropriate and proportionate means). The anger is signalling to us that a personal boundary has been crossed, and we need to act.

On the other hand, if you are feeling particularly happy, it may lead you to be receptive to the seriousness of someone's call for help from you.

So, emotions are not necessarily good or bad. It depends on what they are telling us at the moment and how we react or, better still, respond to them. Emotions are a bit like our in-built sensors – think of them like the parking sensors in your car that help you to know what is happening around you. If, while driving carefully in your car, someone cuts in front of you without warning, your emotional reaction or reflex will hopefully enable you to take control to stay out of harm's way.

When we rely on our natural reactions to a situation, we are doing so with little self control. When we are able to choose our response, that typically leads to better outcomes – think back to the "heaven and hell" Zen parable recounted earlier.

Viktor Frankl, the author of *Man's Search for Meaning*,[2] once said, "Between stimulus and response, there is a space. In that space lies our growth and our freedom."

The key to our experience of life is primarily through our emotions and feelings. These can trigger other thoughts, words we say and actions we take. By developing our own self awareness of our emotions, we can better understand what they are signalling and so exercise our ability to respond or act appropriately.

Better awareness of our emotions enables us to recognise our emotional state. If we do not train our emotional self awareness, we are at risk of overreacting and causing undesirable (and regrettable) results.

How Do You Develop Emotional Self Awareness?

I would strongly recommend that you decide on why you want to do so. Starting with setting your intention on what benefit you can expect to gain will help you to keep putting in continued efforts. You could phrase your intention as follows: "By developing self awareness of my emotions, I can decide how I respond to them."

Feel free to adjust the wording as you see fit. You could tailor it by adding "so that…" and completing it with an important relationship you have (at work or in your personal life) that you want to improve.

With this intention set for why you want to improve self awareness of your emotions, you can then put aside a few minutes daily – preferably when you are alone and free from daily distractions – to reflect on the emotions you felt during the day or the previous day.

Emotional Check-In: Name It to Tame It

Objective: Cultivate awareness and regulation of emotions.

Instructions: Pause at least three times a day and ask, "What am I feeling right now?" Identify and name your feelings. Explore the cause by asking, "What triggered this feeling?" and "What thoughts are tied to this emotion?"

Takeaway: Regularly naming emotions can reduce their intensity and provide clarity.

It is helpful to note down your reflections in a journal, if possible, so that you can revisit and review them in the future should you wish to. You can also choose to not write anything down and just recall recent events in your mind while keeping your eyes closed.

As you develop the habit of noticing recent emotional experiences, you may find yourself being more conscious of your emotions as they emerge during your day's activities. This is a sign of good progress. You notice how you are feeling, and this enables you to respond appropriately.

How you feel will be key in influencing what you communicate to yourself and others. We shall now explore self awareness applied to our words.

Self Awareness of Your Words

As human beings, we have the amazing ability to convey a range of intentions, thoughts, emotions, information and understanding through spoken words (and written ones too).

We do so much more than "grunt"; we use the vast repertoire of words at our disposal. These words are our tools. Like physical tools, we get to choose the ones best suited to the task at hand, and in my humble opinion, we should use them wisely. I believe that choosing our words carefully helps us to set and communicate our intentions with clarity. By intention, I am referring to an aim in mind, whether to establish a connection with someone, to promise or to share thoughts and feelings.

To my mind, words are like arrows. In the Japanese martial art of archery Kyūjutsu (literally the art of the bow 弓術), the practised process focuses entirely on what happens – from setting the intention to the moment the arrow is released. After the arrow is released from the bow, there is nothing more within the practitioner's control that can be done to affect where the arrow lands. Similarly, the arrow, once released, cannot be taken back. Our words, in my view, should not be openly used to injure; they should be deployed with care and precision. We should make our words count. Words that are said cannot be unsaid.

When used carelessly, words are more likely to cause confusion, misunderstanding, offence, fear or hurt.

My belief is that when we pay more attention to the words we use and how we use them, we become better equipped to say them with care and precision. This also applies to the words we say to ourselves!

If you were talking to somebody, what would you notice about the words coming out of your mouth? I do appreciate that this is an odd question, and I ask you to bear with me. What do you notice about the words you say?

Like before, I recommend you develop self awareness of your words. With self awareness, it is important to practice it without self judgement and always with the attitude of curiosity. In effect, self awareness as a practice becomes more of an exploration rather than a driven search for evidence to prove a point!

Take some quiet time to reflect on the day just gone or an event in your day. The key is to start getting curious about how you communicate.

Word Awareness: The Language Audit

Objective: Recognize the impact of your words on yourself and others.

Instructions: For one day, pay close attention to your spoken and written words.

At the end of the day, reflect by journaling, as guided by these questions: "What percentage of my words were positive, neutral, or negative?", "How did my words influence the energy of my interactions?" and "Which areas could you have used more empowering language?"

Takeaway: Identify areas where more intentional, empowering language could be used.

As you become more aware of the words you speak, you will have more control over what you say. In effect, you become more intentional in the way you communicate for the chosen effect. This includes the self talk you have in your mind too. Think of how you feel when you use encouraging words on yourself compared to using hurtful words. We sometimes tend to say hurtful things to ourselves that many of us would not dream of saying to other people! And when I say "we," I include myself here!

Self Awareness of Our Actions

Look back at human history, you'll notice how much of it focuses on what people did, far more than what people said, felt and thought. Actions speak louder than words, after all.

What matters is not so much how great the quality of your thoughts are, the strength of emotion you feel or how competently you communicate; what speaks loudest is what you do. I do not refer to your day job here. I mean the things that you actually do.

I find myself wondering why, when meeting new people at networking events, social occasions or work meetings, people often ask, "What do you do?" It strikes me as a little odd when people used to ask, "How do you do?" at least in spoken English – do what?! People seem more interested in other human beings as "human doings." We act as if we identify each other more by what we do, rather than who we are. In some cultures, the family name you have is related to the family occupation. Think names like "Smith" (English) and "Schmidt" (German), for example. I observe that we, as human beings, are often more preoccupied with what we do than who we are as individuals. Perhaps it is easier for us to answer the enquirer on what we do without getting too deep and personal with a stranger.

There is another angle I'd like to offer here. What we repeatedly do affects who we become. At the time of writing this book, I am keeping an eye (when relaxing) on the sporting spectacle that is the 2024 Olympic Games hosted in Paris. Those amazing athletes did not just decide a week before to start competing; they had spent months, years, to prepare themselves through relentless training and practice. They are not athletes during just the two weeks of the Games, they have been doing what athletes do for some time. While many of you are not Olympic athletes (I'm certainly not!), in a way, we become what we repeatedly do.

Time to do an exercise of self awareness of what you do.

Action Reflection: "The Day in Review"

Objective: Link actions to what is important for me.

Instructions: At the end of each day, reflect on your actions by asking: What did I do today that aligned with what was important for me? What actions felt out of alignment? What small changes could I make tomorrow?

Takeaway: Begin to align daily behaviours more closely with what is important for you.

As before, the key thing to bear in mind with these self awareness reflections is to do so without self judgement. Having said that, I do appreciate that judging ourselves comes very naturally to us, so try to note down when you do before moving on with the awareness exercise anew.

Summary

In this chapter, we explored what self awareness is and why it is important for self improvement. We were introduced to some simple exercises that can help you to enhance your current level of self awareness so that you can start taking back control of the way you live and work.

To change ourselves for the better, we need to first understand where we are now. Self awareness is a deliberate practice to observe ourselves with curiosity and to do so without judgement. This means paying attention to the thoughts we have, the emotions we experience, the words we communicate and the actions we take. With this better understanding, we can decide what to adjust to get improved results.

Why is this so important for you and me? This timeless quote from Lao Tzu captures it all for me!

> "Watch your thoughts, they become your words;
> Watch your words, they become your actions;
> Watch your actions, they become your habits;
> Watch your habits, they become your character;
> Watch your character, it becomes your destiny."

Having started to develop our ability to observe our thoughts, emotions, words and actions, we will move on in the next chapter to improve our understanding of ourselves.

Chapter 2
Self Knowledge
"Know Thyself"

"He who knows others is wise; he who knows himself is enlightened."

– Lao Tzu

The Self-Knowledge Pillar of Personal Mastery

After self awareness – the first pillar on the way to "Taking Back Control" – we will explore self knowledge. Self awareness is the practice of observing your thoughts, feelings, words and actions, while self knowledge is understanding yourself as an individual – recognising your strengths and weaknesses, skills and experiences, as well as your preferences and passions. In this chapter, we will look at what self knowledge is and why it is hugely important for your journey into personal growth. We will also look at a few strategies for helping you develop your self knowledge.

Who are you? In our daily lives, we often find ourselves taking time to get to know others. At a social occasion, it is the accepted custom to ask people we've just met to tell us about themselves. As they speak, we – the ones asking – tend to listen for details that interest us personally. We can learn a lot about those we've just met in these exchanges: their names, professions, who they know and even their likes and dislikes.

An interesting point arrives when we are asked the same question: "Who are you?" How well you respond to the expressed curiosity depends in part on how practised you are in expressing yourself, but more importantly on how well you truly know yourself.

Think of a time when you were applying for a job. During the interview, you were likely requested to talk about yourself. Most job interviews involve you as the candidate responding to queries about yourself and your capabilities. This is because your prospective employers are evaluating whether your mix of qualifications, skills, experience, personality and motivations make you a suitable fit. If you demonstrate a solid understanding and awareness of yourself and your skills, you stand a better chance of securing the role than if you had a less developed understanding of yourself. It is clear from these examples from modern life that having a well-developed level of understanding and acceptance of yourself, i.e. self knowledge, is a worthwhile attribute to cultivate.

Fans of the 1999 science fiction movie *The Matrix* will recall the scene when lead character Neo (Keanu Reeves) goes to consult the altruistic sage known as "The Oracle." Above the doorway at the Oracle's house are the words "tenet nose" – Latin for "know thyself." This is in reference to the ancient Greek Temple of Apollo where high priestess Pythia served as the Oracle of Delphi. Fittingly, in the movie, Neo had questions for the Oracle about his true identity; this was a search for self knowledge after all.

Historically, humankind has always had an appreciation for gaining self knowledge. For Socrates, the goal of philosophy was to "know thyself." The ancient Greek philosopher Aristotle once said, "Knowing oneself is the beginning of all wisdom." Chinese philosopher Lao Tzu is quoted in the *Tao Te Ching*[3] as having said, "Knowing others is intelligence; knowing yourself is true wisdom."

The personal search for self knowledge has a philosophical, even spiritual sense to it, as a point of self discovery. A question arises here as to why this is important to us as individuals. My interpretation is that we, as human beings, ask ourselves the question, "Who am I?" We have an innate desire to gain the most intimate knowledge about ourselves, as it goes towards answering the fundamental question of "Why?"

On a more tangible level, the development of self knowledge allows us to express ourselves to others with clarity and authenticity. We stand to have better success rates of improving a skill or ability if we have a good body of self knowledge. After all, we can't improve what we do not understand.

Traditionally, ways to cultivate a deeper self knowledge involve self reflection, whether by meditating or writing our observations (i.e. journaling). Another way of doing this is to seek help from a coach or mentor who can prompt increased awareness of your current self (think of my earlier movie reference here!). Personally, I have always been drawn to going out on long runs or walks in nature as well as in urban spaces. I describe it as "going somewhere to come back" – a journey that physically returns me to where I started, slightly improved mentally and spiritually. Through meditative practices like running, I gain a little more self knowledge. Other people may get similar returns from other pursuits – playing sports, yoga, martial arts, dance, hiking, diving, swimming, to name a few. These pursuits are linked to finding answers to the "Who am I?" question.

There is a very proactive and practical way to gain a tangible understanding of ourselves. This involves asking yourself a number of questions centred around different themes.

Exercise: Getting To Know You!

Here's a streamlined set of activities for you to explore self knowledge, organized into themes:

Skills and Abilities

You have a unique combination of talent (natural ability) and areas of learned expertise (acquired skill).

Action: Reflect and write your answers to these questions.

- What are your top three skills in your professional and personal life?
- What skills do others recognise in you? Ask someone for feedback!
- What do you excel at or feel confident doing?

Strengths and Weaknesses

You have both areas of competence and less competence. Some strengths can also become weaknesses if overused.

Action: Identify and balance your qualities.

- List three key strengths.
- List three key weaknesses.
- Which strengths could also be weaknesses, and vice versa?

Interests and Passions

You have specific areas of interest and some that you are enthusiastic about.

Action: Define what lights you up.

- What are your top three interests at work and in life?
- What hobbies or passions bring you joy?
- How do you spend your leisure time?

Values and Aspirations

You have principles that you adhere to. You have hopes and dreams for your future.

Action: Reflect on your purpose and vision.

- What are your three most important values?
- Are you living in alignment with them?
- Where do you see yourself in 10 years? (Consider achievements, personal growth, and contributions to the world.)

Key Life Experiences

You go through life accumulating experiences. Some of these experiences are especially memorable for you and shape the person you are today. These become the stories that you tell yourself and others.

Action: Recall transformative moments.

- Write down your top life experiences. Three to five will do.
- What made these moments significant for you?

Personality Profile

A personality profile contains a set of psychological characteristics that speak of the way you perceive, evaluate, communicate and behave. Carl Jung's theory of psychological types identified 16 distinct natural personality types. An increased awareness of your personality traits means you can understand yourself more and perform at your best. This also helps you to understand natural psychological differences between yourself and others.

Based on empirical evidence and Carl Jung's work, Isabel Myers Briggs developed a tool called the Myers Briggs Type Indicator® (MBTI®), which helps to identify a person's personality type by their responses to several prescribed questions.[4,5] The following are some very topline questions that investigate the Myers-Briggs personality type you may have, but typically, an MBTI® will pose more extensive questions.

Action: Understand your traits using these prompts.

- Are you more extroverted (E) or introverted (I)?
- Do you focus on facts (S) or the big picture (N)?
- Are your decisions based on logic (T) or personal values (F)?
- Do you prefer planning (J) or spontaneity (P)?

Tip: Use a Myers-Briggs Type Indicator® tool for deeper insights (see Resources section).

Character

You have a personality that is made up of how you conduct yourself with respect to ethical, moral and social attitudes and beliefs.

Action: Define who you are.

- What five words describe your personality?
- Ask someone you trust how they would describe you.

Self Identity

Who are you? This is a question for deep self reflection. This is to get to know who you are beneath external conventions (e.g. social, environmental).

Action: Go deeper into self reflection.

- Who am I when I am alone?
- How do I feel and act in solitude?

Self knowledge is a journey, not a one-time activity. Revisit these exercises periodically. As you grow, your answers may evolve, providing new insights into who you are and who you aspire to be.

You may be thinking, "That is a lot of questions!" I get it. Many of them are not necessarily easy ones either. Who said self knowledge was easy?! If it were a case of picking up a book and reading it, then perhaps everyone would do it (or would they?). The pursuit of self knowledge is a continual practice. You may return to these same questions from time to time. Your answers may change too, especially as you are changing over time, in your understanding, experiences and abilities.

On the other hand, we have so far only scratched the surface through the questions posed on each of the eight aspects of self knowledge. To go deeper, you'll find additional supporting resources in the Resources section of this book.

An Alternative Approach to Improving Self Knowledge

Many of the approaches I have shared to develop self knowledge have been centred on self reflection. There is an alternative approach which merits inclusion here: gaining self knowledge through taking action. Arriving at an encyclopedic knowledge of ourselves is one thing; it is quite another when we gain experiential knowledge of ourselves. It is by doing and putting into practice what is known academically that makes self knowledge powerful.

Applying what we know about ourselves in practice leads to deeper self knowledge. In fact, I intend for this book to be practical. It is in the application that true personal growth is to be found.

Self Knowledge

It is usually said that practice makes perfect, when in reality, "practice makes progress." I have borrowed this phrase from memory expert Jim Kwik, who also said, "Knowledge is not power; knowledge is only potential power – it becomes power when you use it." That is an insightful quote!

Consider how it is that we read so many books and take so many courses – consuming so much material – and yet have nothing to show for it. It is one thing to say you've read a book and quite another to show what you learned from it. I like to challenge others by saying, "Show me, don't tell me!" Of course, not every personal development book that you come across will be what you are looking for or indeed be right for you at that point in time. We can choose to discern what we want to retain and what to discard.

Another way to gain experiential self knowledge is by doing things outside of your comfort zone. Some of these experiences have turned out to be what I call "defining moments" – turning points that have moulded me into the person I am today. They serve as meaningful milestones in my journey that I can choose to share with others when explaining who I am. I share one such defining moment here. Perhaps it may prompt you to recall your defining moments.

One day, early on in my pharmaceutical career, I was attending an on-site end-of-year company meeting. From the stage, the CEO of our company presented the year's performance results. I was among around 2,000 colleagues in attendance. As the presentation progressed, I was struck by the CEO's omission of vaccines, which was a third arm of the company's business and happened to be the part within which I worked.

I was passionate about the role that vaccines play in global health, especially in the developing world. So when it was time for questions, my arm shot up for the opportunity. Sure enough, I was the first employee to be handed the microphone. Nervously, I looked at the CEO on the stage, introduced myself and asked whether he could talk about the part of the business I was in, given the omission that I noticed. I'll never forget his reply. "Well, Jung," he said, "I only spoke of the blockbuster products, the ones that performed well. Quite frankly, Jung, you've just got to work harder!" At the CEO's reply, all 2,000 people joined in to laugh at me. I felt like I had been kicked squarely in the stomach. My heart pounded uncontrollably. I could hardly breathe. My mind swirled with disbelief, confusion, anguish, despair and pain all at once. I was on the verge of collapsing on the spot.

Then I heard a little voice whispering, "You are still holding the mic!" Slowly but surely, after what seemed like an eternity, I held tighter onto the microphone, stood up straight, and regained my gaze at the CEO on the stage. The world went quiet. My words came to me. "That's all very well. While our business faces constraints like manufacturing capacity, vaccines continue to play a major role in global health initiatives, especially in the developing world." The CEO relented. He spoke about how he was aware of the challenges and had even had dinner with Bill and Melinda Gates to discuss vaccination programmes. I recovered by speaking my words. I felt stronger inside. For the first time I can recall, I stood up for myself!

After this experience, no further mention was made of it, not even by my manager; I still kept my job. Around two weeks later, I happened to look up from my desk in the open-plan office, and my eyes met with the CEO. He was walking through our offices. I nodded just as he nodded back in acknowledgement. Perhaps it was a way of showing mutual respect. No doubt he remembered me. Nothing more was said nor needed to be.

Since that time, I have taken the opportunity to ask any CEO or leader my questions. Whatever you may think of the appropriateness of the CEO's reply to me in my anecdote, I have taken the experience to learn about myself. I learned that I can stand up for myself and speak my truth. I learned the value of courage. After all, if I do not stand up for myself, who will?

Summary

We have an innate desire to answer the question, "Who am I?" The more we explore our own abilities, experiences, preferences, aspirations and perspectives, the clearer and more informed our answer to this most fundamental of questions will be. And surely that can only be a good thing.

I recommend spending around 15 minutes a week mulling over one or two of the questions in this chapter and noting your findings. You may also look back at what you have discovered so far. Over time, you will get to know yourself with greater clarity.

In this chapter, we looked at what self knowledge is and why it is important as a component of self improvement. We have covered some questions to help you gain a deeper understanding of yourself.

In the next chapter, we will look at the pillar of self management, which, when combined with the earlier pillars of self awareness and self knowledge, ensures that you can take back control for yourself so that you can do your best work and live better each day.

"Your visions will become clear only when you can look into your own heart. Who looks outside, dreams; who looks inside, awakes."

– Carl Jung

Chapter 3
Self Management
"Taking Self Ownership"

"You can't pour from an empty cup. Take care of yourself first."

– Unknown

The Self-Management Pillar of Personal Mastery

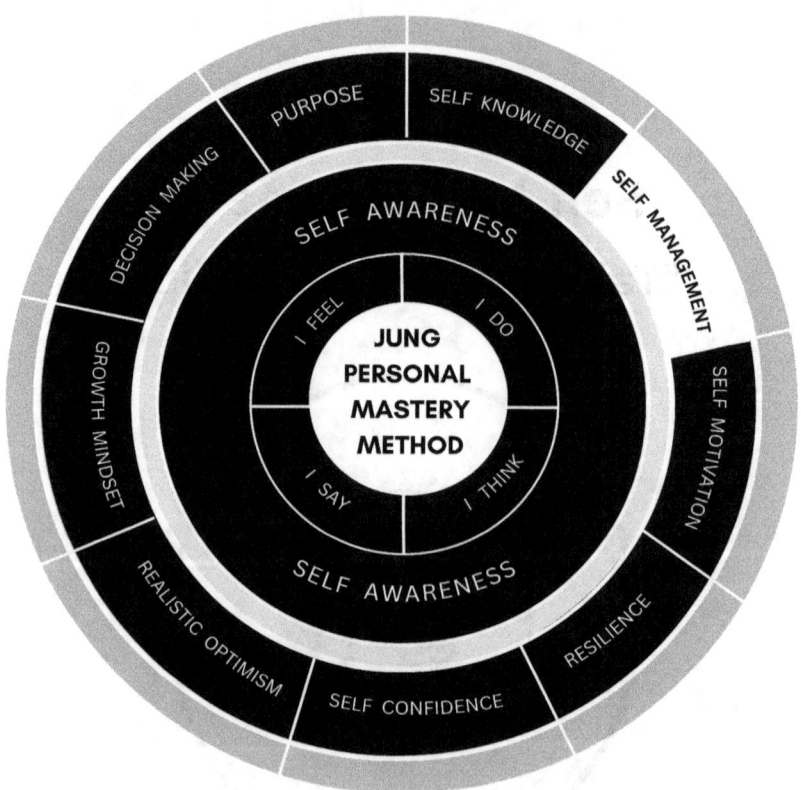

So far, we have taken the journey to observe how we react and respond, and just now get to know who we are. This journey is not linear by any stretch, the work continues with revisiting self awareness and self knowledge to keep evolving. For us to be able to take control of our lives, the next step is to apply what we know and understand about ourselves so that we can maintain optimal conditions. This chapter is not just about gaining understanding, it involves taking action to realise "Taking Back Control" for ourselves. It is through being in our best condition that we can achieve more and grow. It is through what I call self management that we take full ownership of ourselves and direct ourselves to achieve and grow.

The optimal condition is one where we are in balance between opposites. Rather than working or resting 100% of the time, we stay somewhere in between the extremes. Similarly, rather than being active or passive 100% of the time when it comes to our involvement in work projects, we should be somewhere in between. Note that the exact line between the extremes is constantly moving.

In this way, the balance is a dynamic one that adjusts accordingly. What works well in one situation may need adjustment to adapt to the needs of another. This equilibrium is dynamic or constantly changing.

Perspective: Through the Lens of Yin and Yang

The symbol at the start of this chapter may appear familiar to some of you. It is the "Yin Yang" symbol from Chinese Taoist philosophy and speaks of a universal principle. The two opposing forces are called Yin and Yang. In simplified Chinese, Yin (阴) [yīn] is represented by the character for the moon, while Yang (阳) [yáng] is represented by the sun character. Yin is associated with decreasing, retracting, receiving, dropping, dark, cold, soft, smooth, feminine, negative and non-linear, while Yang is associated with increasing, expanding, giving, rising, light, heat, hard, rough, masculine, positive and linear. These are only natural characteristics and not labelled as good or bad per se – what is important is the overall balance between the two.

The diagram consists of two "tadpole shapes" of equal size and proportion. They are equal and opposite forces of change. Each part of Yin has a little Yang within and vice versa. This reflects the dynamic nature of change – every shift toward increasing Yang is accompanied by simultaneously decreasing Yin, gradually increasing until Yin becomes more dominant. Likewise, every shift toward increasing Yin is accompanied by simultaneously decreasing Yang.

A system in a predominant Yin state of change does not remain Yin indefinitely; it naturally transitions into Yang. Similarly, a system in a predominantly Yang state does not remain so permanently, it will eventually shift into Yin.

This continuous cycle can be likened to the ebb and flow of ocean waves. The incoming waves (Yang) do not come indefinitely. There will be a natural point at which those same waves will lose momentum and will start to recede back to the sea (Yin).

Self Management

To help you understand this, let's illustrate it through breathing. We naturally inhale and exhale repeatedly. Inhalation could be considered a Yang movement because the lungs need to expand to bring in air. Consider that your lungs will, at some point, reach their maximum capacity for taking in air, resulting in the Yin influence taking over. As you expel air, your lungs will once again reach a point where they can deflate no longer – and Yang comes back in.

You may notice with this illustration that the act of lungs breathing out feels more Yang in nature than Yin. And you are onto something. It depends on what you are considering. Expelling air out of the body from the lungs is a Yang movement (pushing air outwards), while the act of drawing air into the lungs is a Yin movement (receiving air inwards).

A river would not flow if there was no spring located higher up than the sea. An electrical current would not flow if there was no positive or negative charge. Processes with a natural cycle can be seen through the lens of Yin and Yang.

Early in the morning, for example, you may feel more Yang because of increasing energy to perform and work. By the late evening, you may feel more Yin because of decreasing Yang energy and feel the need to recuperate (recharge). Both Yang and Yin phases have their part to play.

The idea of the dynamic interplay between Yin and Yang is what we observe in the world around us and in our bodies. The idea of homeostasis, which is how the body keeps processes running in dynamic balance, fits in with this concept. When this state of dynamic balance risks being severely disrupted, then the way the body naturally functions is affected, and the state of flow needs to be restored. This concept of a dynamic balance is what I want you to bear in mind as we progress through what we explore next in this chapter.

Self Care

The pillar of self management can be encapsulated as "self care." For a deeper understanding, I recommend you consult the abundance of literature and resources available and your physician as appropriate.

Self care can be thought of as self maintenance. Imagine your car fails to start on your way to work. Why? Is there fuel in the tank or has the battery drained up? Is there sufficient lubrication or oil to ensure the parts move smoothly? These and other questions may come to mind. You may start kicking yourself for not having the car serviced regularly as was recommended. If you don't look after your own car, at some point, it is likely to perform at less than its best. We are far more intricate and complex than a car. Good, consistent self maintenance is part of self care and essential for good functioning and performance.

The practice of self care is certainly not new. Being living creatures, we need to ensure that our basic needs are met. Food, water, air, rest and sleep are a given. When we lack any one of these, we find out pretty quickly why they are important. When we have too much of any, there are detrimental effects too. This points to the somewhat crude cliché, "moderation is key." The problem with this cliché is that it suggests a little bit of everything is OK, giving license to ingest foods that do more harm than good, even in small quantities.

In fact, if you refer to Abraham Maslow's Hierarchy of Needs[6], these earlier listed factors make up the lowest tier of needs – the most essential for our day-to-day survival and existence. Abraham Maslow devised his hierarchy of needs within motivational psychology to represent the ones necessary to function optimally. He placed the most important needs for survival, i.e. physiological needs, at the bottom tier of the hierarchy. These need to be met before the higher-tier ones can be reached. We are motivated in life to have these human needs met to some degree.

Abraham Maslow's Hierarchy of Needs

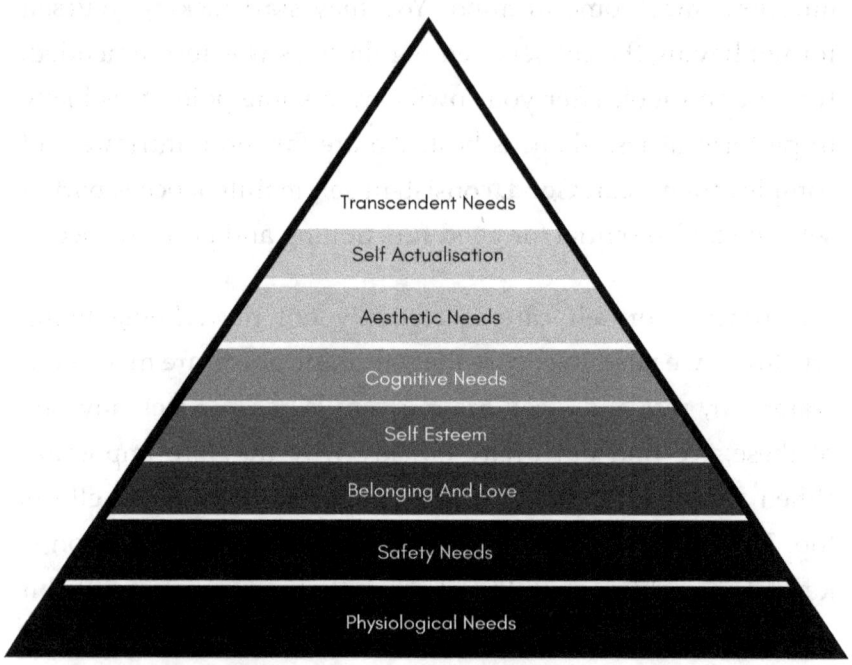

Physiological Needs

In extreme cases, the human body can go without sleep and rest for days. We can survive days without food, but we cannot survive for as long without water. If you were to stop breathing, you would not last more than a couple of minutes (I do not suggest you try this unless under expert instruction). The human body does what it does with brilliant efficiency, keeping all physiological processes they should in balance.

I trust that as you are reading this, you are nowhere near the extremes just outlined. However, how optimally are your physiological needs normally met? If they are not consistently being well met, then over time, this can lead to future problems in your health and affect your quality of life.

You may find that you often wake up feeling tired and reluctant to get started on the day ahead. You may be hungry and sluggish shortly after meals. You may not be feeling the need to urinate as often as you should – or a combination of all these!

Here are some exercises to stimulate more awareness of how well you are meeting your physiological needs:

Sleep and Rest

Awareness: How rested do you typically feel after a night of rest?

Strategy: What is one thing you can do to ensure you get better sleep in both quality and quantity? You could go to bed earlier, refrain from social media or TV before bed, allow at least two hours between the last meal of the day and bedtime etc.

Implementation: Apply your chosen strategy and measure how you feel each day over two weeks. Adjust strategy for optimal results.

Diet

Awareness: How would you rate the health and balance of your diet in terms of vegetables and fruit, protein (such as meat, fish or plant-based sources), and carbohydrates (like potatoes, pasta, bread or rice)?

Strategy: What is one thing you can do to ensure you get a more healthy and balanced diet? You could include more vegetables and fruits in your meals, cut down on carbohydrates and sugar, reduce alcohol intake etc.

Implementation: Apply your chosen strategy and measure how you feel each day over two weeks. Adjust strategy for optimal results.

Hydration

Awareness: How much water do you drink each day?

Strategy: What is one thing you can do to ensure you improve the amount of water you drink? You could try drinking a glass of water first thing in the morning and the like.

Implementation: Apply your chosen strategy and measure how you feel each day over two weeks. Adjust strategy for optimal results.

Breathing

Awareness: How would you describe your breathing throughout the day? Is it shallow or deep? Is it rapid or slow?

Strategy: What is one thing you can do to ensure you improve your breathing? You could try paying attention to your breathing at least twice a day, slow down your breathing for a full minute etc.

Implementation: Apply your chosen strategy and measure how you feel each day over two weeks. Adjust strategy for optimal results.

Safety Needs

Above the tier of our most essential needs – physiological needs – the next priority is our need for safety. This includes health, personal security and emotional security. People generally want to have order, economic predictability and control in their lives. These needs are often met through family support and societal structures, such as community services, welfare, housing, and healthcare. Additionally, people require protection from physical dangers and environmental threats, as well as safeguards against occupational hazards.

If you find that you have your safety needs met, then you are among the fortunate. Many people around the world face challenges with having their safety needs met, especially when conflict and political instability come into play.

Awareness: In what area of your life do you feel you need more safety or security?

Strategy: What is one thing you can do to ensure you improve this for you?

Implementation: Apply your chosen strategy and measure how well it works for you.

Belonging and Love

The first two tiers in the hierarchy, physiological and safety needs, make up our most necessary needs – "basic needs." After meeting these basic needs, there is belonging and love. This speaks to our need for interpersonal social connection: intimate relationships, friendships, connections with other people etc. The sense of belonging brings with it the feeling of being comfortable with others, accompanied by connection. This leads to receiving acceptance, interpersonal respect and love. Being in social groups like clubs, faith groups, with co-workers and teams, or having life partners and mentors are a few examples of where the belonging and love needs may be met. The absence of love and belonging can lead to people feeling loneliness and social anxiety.

Awareness: In what area of your life do you feel you need more belonging and love?

Strategy: What is one thing you can do to ensure you improve this for yourself?

Implementation: Apply your chosen strategy and measure how well it works for you.

Self Esteem Needs

After belonging and love comes self esteem needs. This is respect and admiration from others, as well as self respect. Confidence, achievement and the need to be a unique individual lie here. It is one thing to be esteemed by others, but it is not especially healthy if we become dependent on it. The accumulation of positive self-learning experiences from both successes and failures inevitably helps the individual concerned to develop a sense of self (self knowledge), which encourages better self esteem.

Awareness: In what area of your life do you feel you could have a good level of self esteem?

Strategy: What is one thing you can do to help you apply this to other areas of your life?

Implementation: Apply your chosen strategy and measure how well it works for you.

Cognitive Needs

Cognitive needs come next. These include creativity, foresight, curiosity, understanding and meaning. Some people will express a more pronounced cognitive need than others, driving them to engage in deliberate creative or intellectual pursuits.

Awareness: In what area of your life do you feel you could have your cognitive needs met?

Strategy: What is one thing you can do to ensure you meet these needs?

Implementation: Apply your chosen strategy and measure how well it works for you.

Aesthetic Needs

After cognitive needs are aesthetic needs. This is a need that comes from creating beauty or looking for and appreciating beauty. Beauty can be found in nature, in the world we live in, appreciating art and not forgetting it is within ourselves and other people. It can refer to the beauty of balance and form. Where one sees and experiences this is entirely subjective – "Beauty is in the eye of the beholder," so the saying goes.

Awareness: In what area of your life do you feel you could meet your need for aesthetics?

Strategy: What is one thing you can do to ensure you meet these needs?

Implementation: Apply your chosen strategy and measure how well it works for you.

Self Actualisation

Maslow succinctly captured the concept of self actualisation when he said, "What you can become, you must become." This is the need that humans have for realising self potential, self fulfilment and the search for personal growth and peak experiences. I think of it as becoming the best version of ourselves.

I recall asking personal growth expert and author Robin Sharma about his greatest fears at a talk once, and his reply was unforgettable: "leaving potential unexpressed." That speaks of the desire to fully meet the need for self actualisation. How often do you notice people, ourselves included, who have traded away their full genius, passions and talents?

Awareness: In what area of your life do you feel you could meet your need for self actualisation?

Strategy: What is one thing you can do to ensure you meet this need?

Implementation: Apply your chosen strategy and measure how well it works for you.

Transcendence Needs

Many people are familiar with the human need for self actualisation – to become our best selves, achieving personal growth and fulfilment. One of the more recent additions to Maslow's hierarchy of needs includes transcendence needs. This relates to the human desire to go beyond self actualisation, to connect to a higher purpose or reality. Altruism, spiritual connection and helping others to achieve this potential are about transcendent needs. They are typically about meeting needs beyond personal concerns. Examples include cultivating religious faith or other spiritual practices, service to others and pursuing scientific understanding.

The psychological idea that self transcendence is a central feature of the healthy individual was first described by Viktor Frank[17]. As Maslow[7] said, "Transcendence refers to the very highest and the most inclusive or holistic levels of human consciousness, behaving and relating, as ends rather than means, to oneself, to significant others, to human beings in general, to other species, to nature and to the cosmos."

Awareness: What draws you to help others?

Strategy: What is one thing you can do to ensure you do more to help others?

Implementation: Apply your chosen strategy and measure how well it works for you.

Limitations of the Maslow Hierarchy of Needs Model

Having explored Maslow's hierarchy of needs, it is tempting to think that it explains everything we need to know about the types of needs humans have and the relative order of priority. It gives the impression that one must fully meet the needs of each "lower tier" before progressing to the next more complex higher need. It serves as a convenient model to reflect on but requires some caveats to be applicable. Having food and water does not guarantee good health; you need to look at the diet and quality of the food and water. It is also possible to partly satisfy your transcendent needs without meeting the more basic ones.

When we talk about self management, we are not only advised to consider the needs we have to satisfy but also to ensure we practise self regulation. No overconsumption of food, nutrients or the wrong types of food, for example. This self regulation or management is not a single activity but a regular practice to ensure you are at your optimal state.

In my view, the hierarchy of needs presented by Maslow is a comprehensive overview. However, it can be overwhelming if we try to put the concepts into practical use on a day-to-day basis. For a simpler way to go about meeting our needs while maintaining good self management, I recommend grouping our overall needs into the following four categories. Below, you will also find real-life examples.

Physical Needs

Your physical needs relate to maintaining your physical health. They are the basic requirements that must be met to sustain life, health and well-being. They form the foundation of human survival and include the essentials for maintaining the body's functionality and overall physical health. They make up the first level in Maslow's Hierarchy of Needs.

Overwork and poor wellness routines are examples of physical needs at risk of not being met. Work could be considered a Yang activity, and wellness or rest a Yin activity.

Arianna Huffington (co-founder of The Huffington Post, founder and CEO of Thrive Global and author of fifteen books) – Burnout and Collapse

Arianna Huffington's intense work schedule led to a physical collapse in her office, where she broke her cheekbone. This event prompted her to reevaluate her lifestyle. She began prioritising sleep, meditation and setting boundaries around work. She later wrote Thrive[8], advocating for well-being as a measure of success.

Lesson: Recognizing the signals of physical exhaustion and making lifestyle changes not only restore health but also enhance performance and joy.

Reflection: What signs of physical exhaustion do you recognise in your daily life?

Emotional Needs

This need is all about your emotional health. These are the core feelings and experiences that you require to feel emotionally balanced, secure and fulfilled. Meeting these needs helps you maintain mental and emotional well-being, build meaningful relationships and navigate life's challenges with resilience.

Managing stressful relationships and rediscovering joy in work are examples of where people may want to focus on to meet their emotional needs.

Barack Obama (former US President) – Staying Emotionally Grounded

Barack Obama's presidency was marked by composure and emotional intelligence, even during turbulent times. He managed his emotional needs by spending quality time with his family, maintaining close friendships and regularly reflecting through journaling and prayer. His ability to connect with people empathetically was a key factor of his leadership style.

Lesson: A strong emotional foundation, built through relationships and reflection, allows leaders to navigate high-pressure situations with grace.

Reflection: What are the key relationships in your own life? How would your life improve if your key relationships were stronger?

Mental Needs

Your mental needs refer to your mental health. This means maintaining cognitive well-being, clarity, and a sense of control over your thoughts and decision-making. Meeting these needs fosters intellectual growth, problem-solving abilities and emotional resilience. Mental needs are essential for navigating complex challenges, maintaining focus and feeling capable in life and work.

Feeling overwhelmed and living with limiting beliefs are examples where mental needs are not being addressed.

Bill Gates (American businessman and philanthropist best known for co-founding Microsoft) – Lifelong Learning

Bill Gates is a staunch advocate for continuous learning as a way to stay mentally sharp. He dedicates time to reading extensively, attending think-tank events and reflecting on global challenges. His well-documented "Think Weeks," where he isolates himself to read and strategize, highlight his commitment to mental clarity and innovation.

Lesson: Taking intentional time for focused learning and reflection can expand mental horizons and enhance decision-making.

Reflection: What do you currently do to make time for learning and reflection?

Spiritual Needs

Your spiritual needs refer to the deep, often intangible requirements that help individuals find purpose, meaning and connection. These needs go beyond physical, mental and emotional aspects, focusing on aligning with your values, higher purpose or a sense of something greater than oneself. Spiritual needs vary among individuals based on beliefs, values and experiences, but they are fundamental to personal fulfilment and inner peace.

Feeling unfulfilled at work and feeling lost in life are some examples of lacking spiritual needs.

Maya Angelou (American memoirist, poet, and civil rights activist) – Grounded in Faith and Self Expression

Maya Angelou addressed her spiritual needs through faith, poetry and storytelling. Her works, infused with themes of resilience and hope, reflect a life deeply rooted in spiritual exploration and alignment with her truth. She often credited her faith and connection to humanity as sources of strength.

Lesson: Exploring and expressing spirituality through creative and reflective practices can deepen self awareness and purpose.

Reflection: What does fulfilment mean to you?

An Alternative Way of Looking at Human Needs

Stephen R. Covey, author of *The 7 Habits of Highly Effective People*, referred to the four basic human needs above as "To live, to love, to learn, to leave a legacy" in his book *First Things First*.[9] What I like about this expression is that it describes these not just as "needs" but as capacities. For example, we have physiological needs to live, but we can also thrive to live more fully with vitality and energy so long as the basic need is more than met. Think how useful you would be if you barely had enough to eat, just enough water to drink and just enough sleep every day – not useful to yourself, or indeed to anyone else, I'd say.

My intention here is to highlight a few principles to help you maintain your own optimal health levels in each of these four areas. I'll share strategies and examples to help you decide what works best for you. Just because a given strategy works for me does not mean it is guaranteed to suit you.

It is important to ask yourself what your current level of health is in each area and what level of improvement you are looking to get. Also worth bearing in mind is that a gain in one area will lead

Physical Health

Air (Oxygen)

Breathing is a physical action that we do not need to think about, it is autonomous and involuntary. We don't usually need to remind ourselves to inhale and exhale – a fortunate fact, as a constant supply of oxygen is essential to prevent organ failure. However, when we focus on our breathing, we can temporarily control it until our awareness shifts and the body›s natural rhythm takes over again.

An important factor in our physical health is the quality of air we breathe. Air pollution in busy urban areas is a major cause of poor respiratory health. Cities like London have imposed traffic speed and volume restrictions to curb air pollution from fossil-fuel-burning vehicles. Taking walks in parks and woodlands is a good way of ensuring better air intake as part of good daily self management.

Another point I'd highlight is being conscious of how you breathe. Do you breathe normally through your mouth or your nose? Nasal breathing appears to be better for health.[10] Do you breathe through your abdomen or your chest? Abdominal breathing is associated with deeper breathing and makes better use of your natural lung capacity.

Water

After air, water is the next most important factor for the body's self care. The human body is composed of around 60% water, but it is used for nearly all bodily functions, including digestion, temperature regulation and waste elimination. This means water is constantly being lost from the body.

Good water intake is essential to maintain optimal levels. In terms of daily water intake, the UK government recommends 1.2 litres for adults (that's 6 to 8 glasses). However, the actual amount depends on physical activity level, temperature, age and health condition. If you exercise heavily in hot conditions, you are likely to need to make a bigger effort to replenish lost fluids.

Food

The saying "You are what you eat" has a degree of truth to it. It is worth being mindful of what and how much food you eat. The body needs nutrients from food for energy and materials for growth, maintenance and repair – these include macronutrients in the form of carbohydrates (energy), proteins (building blocks) and fats (energy and function) and micronutrients in the form of vitamins and minerals needed for bodily functions. Each individual will have a unique mix of requirements for each nutrient, depending on metabolism rate, age, sex, activity levels etc. Normally, the body is able to take what it needs from food ingested. Excesses are either stored or excreted as appropriate. Sugars and starches can be converted into fats for energy storage in the body.

Taking Back Control

There is a wealth of advice on food and nutrition, with most data focusing on regions known as "blue zones" where people tend to live longer and healthier lives. One key observation is that their diets primarily consist of fresh vegetables, with only small amounts of meat or other protein sources. Note that both excesses and deficiencies can negatively impact health, and consuming fewer processed foods generally benefits overall well-being. In modern society, carbohydrate-rich foods – such as sugars and starches – are widely available, but excessive consumption has been linked to metabolic diseases like diabetes and obesity. Additionally, food intolerances, such as those to dairy or gluten, can lead to digestive issues.

Beyond considering what to eat, it is worth being mindful of when you eat. Heavy meals require a lot of energy to digest, so overeating can leave us feeling sluggish. Eating close to bedtime can mean food does not get digested properly with unintended consequences to health. Some nutritionists recommend restricting the time window of each day for meals – intermittent fasting – with some reporting feeling more energy when practised. As always, such practices should be done with caution and with medical advice as appropriate.

When we find ourselves ravenously hungry (the term "hangry" comes to mind!), we may have an urge to raid the fridge or larder. We are then less likely to opt for the fresh green salad and instead go for the fatty snack or sugary chocolate bar.

I consider myself fairly mindful of the food I eat. Having said that, I do overeat at times too. Nobody's perfect! On most mornings, I will have a vegetable smoothie (without fruit) to boost my daily intake of greens. I try to keep my consumption of processed food low. Generally, I am not super restrictive on my dietary choices, as I want to feel good about the food I eat. I also note that I am less inclined to indulge in food that will leave me feeling sluggish and unwell.

Sleep

Good sleep is an important daily habit. With impaired or insufficient sleep, our alertness and performance capabilities will suffer. During sleep, the body repairs itself, grows muscles and regulates hormones while the brain consolidates memories. When chronic sleep deprivation occurs, severe health problems can arise.

Sleep experts recommend 7 to 8 hours of continuous sleep daily as sufficient, but age can affect this. There is evidence that people may have different sleeping time preferences. Some of you are inclined to be early risers, while others are definitely not. You have the skylarks and the night owls among you.

Sleep is best achieved when we feel relaxed and free from anxiety. For this reason, refraining from the following before bedtime is advisable: engaging in social media, watching and listening to the news, watching violent or traumatising movies, checking work emails etc.

Disorders like sleep apnea and insomnia are best tackled with medical support, as chronic sleep deprivation is bad for health.

Physical Activity

"To exercise or not to exercise?" That is the question. Indeed, why exercise? Stepping back for a moment, think of how the human body is structured for movement, to walk in a bipedal fashion, with arms and hands that can carry or manipulate objects or be used for self defence. If you and I were living with our ancestors of 50,000 years ago, our daily lives would be full of physical activities: hunting, gathering food, preparing food and doing other chores without the modern machinery and gadgetry we are now accustomed to. Movement, lifting, pulling and pushing would be a natural part of life, making extra exercise unnecessary – unless, of course, we were training for a competition!

Thanks to our modern lifestyles, many of us are stationary for hours each day: sitting at the desk in front of our computer screens and devices, riding vehicles to get from point A to B etc. This leaves us with underused muscles and ligaments, poor posture and skeletal weakness. Without exercise, we would be unable to move faster than a walking pace or lift anything heavier than what we are used to. Due to our comparatively sedentary lifestyle, there is an imperative to develop our physical fitness in order to do more and do it better.

Our capacity to perform strenuous physical activity declines with age. Although there are outliers, with older individuals who can retain and develop such physical strength, stamina and suppleness that would shame youngsters decades younger! Your desired fitness level depends on what you want. Being able to run an endurance event like a marathon may not be right for everyone.

The same can be said for being able to lift more than your own body weight unless you want to be an Olympic weightlifter!

Physical exercises that develop strength include using weights (including your own body weight, such as in my favoured activity, callisthenics). Endurance or stamina building involves exercises that are lower in intensity but have longer duration (e.g. running, cycling and swimming). Suppleness can be enhanced through slow or deliberate exercises meant to improve the degree of movement of limbs and your back, for example.

These three broad factors for fitness, called the "3 S's" – Strength, Stamina, Suppleness – are a good guide to help you determine the suitable type and quantity of exercise right for you. Beyond being beneficial in those areas, exercise can help develop physical coordination, maintain cardiovascular health, promote relaxation and improve metabolic rate. Exercise can be great at increasing energy levels. When you are feeling a little sluggish, a short burst of physical movement can give a good boost of energy. Personally, my physical practices of choice are martial arts, running and callisthenics. I have found that the more I practice, the more attuned I am with my own physical state. I am of the view that the same will apply to the physical exercise you do too.

Emotional Health

"To experience peace does not mean that your life is always blissful. It means that you are capable of tapping into a blissful state of mind amidst the normal chaos of a hectic life."

– Jill Bolte Taylor

For most of my corporate career, I had a long commute between home and the office. In the mornings, I managed this by leaving before the morning rush, but at the end of the work day, I would get caught up in heavy commuter traffic. I would spend a total of three hours daily commuting, and I consistently worked at the office from Monday to Friday! My martial arts teacher remarked that I was likely accumulating a lot of stress this way. I dismissed this observation at the time because I thought I was making good use of the time by listening to educational podcasts. It was only later that I realised I was often feeling worked up, stressed and tired whenever I arrived home to my family, who would then be on the receiving end of my poor emotional state. Fortunately, I learned to adjust my commute so that I would be in a better emotional state for my family and colleagues!

Our emotional health and well-being rely on our ability to recognize our feelings, understand our emotional state and take action to regulate it. If we consistently feel excessive stress in a given situation, it is in our interest to regulate ourselves emotionally through understanding, not suppression. Remember that sustained repressed negative emotional states can be bad for physical health and well-being.

When we are considering a challenging problem, we need to regulate our emotional state in order to think objectively and determine the optimal strategy. Conversely, when we are handling a sensitive event like a bereavement, we may need to be attuned and empathetic to the emotional support needed by others.

When we are in the moment, carried along by our emotional state (it happens), we are helpless – until we break out of it and reset. Resetting can be done in a number of ways. One simple, powerful technique is pausing and taking a long, deep breath. This has the effect of reinvigorating us physiologically and helps regulate our sympathetic nervous system and stimulate our parasympathetic nervous system. This has the result of helping us to return to a state of calm. Similarly, practices such as meditation and reflection help too.

We can choose to look for the positive even when things look negative. We can choose to exercise gratitude instead of jealousy and resentment. This enables us to see possibilities rather than fixed or closed dead ends.

Another component of emotional well-being is in the social dimension of our lives. Your relationships with yourself, your life partner, family, friends, peers and neighbours all affect our emotional life, whether you permit it or not. Looking for ways to improve these relationships or only nurture the ones most important to you will make it better in the long run.

Mental Health

"The happiness of your life depends on the quality of your thoughts."
— Marcus Aurelius

The term "mental health" is widely used and, in some definitions, broadly includes emotional well-being. Here, I will treat mental well-being as pertaining to our psychology, beliefs, discipline, problem solving and creativity. A lot of this is down to our mindset, i.e. how we think and rationalise and how well we cognitively understand ourselves and the world.

Poor mental health can arise when people are not constantly learning, growing, gaining new interesting perspectives, acquiring new skills or developing existing skills. When we perform these well, we have a thriving mindset, and our mental health will improve.

The quality of our mental life is key to determining our ability to perform – consider the words of Marcus Aurelius above. Noticing the quality of our thoughts is powerful as this gives us feedback to make use of. It is of further value to realise that you and I can, with intention, make deliberate steps towards improving the quality of our thoughts. We can therefore upgrade our mental programming to more effectively operate, respond, create, communicate and make sense of events past and present.

When I quoted Stephen Covey[9] earlier in this chapter, the "L" pertaining to mental health was "learning". Throughout my personal growth journey, I have always been inclined to learn new things. I enjoyed reading to improve my understanding and knowledge. I was drawn to acquiring new skills that I thought were interesting and useful, including learning different languages and speed reading. I later realised that learning can go deeper or broader depending on what I was interested in.

Learning about a subject of personal interest, whether for professional reasons or more leisure-orientated pursuits, can be career and life-enhancing. The way that the mentioned learning takes place, especially if suited to your learning style, can prove impactful. Proactive learning exercises the brain, enabling the brain to form and strengthen neural connections.

Acquiring a new skill is a great way to improve mental health, especially if there is a degree of difficulty in gaining it. Consider the challenge a non-musician learning to play the guitar would have compared to a musician who already plays another stringed instrument. As an enthusiast who speaks French and Spanish with a reasonable level of fluency, the cognitive challenge of learning Korean is much greater than it would be if I was, say, learning another Latin language.

Another way to enhance mental health is to seek and get novel experiences. Travelling abroad or to other places nationally are great ways of doing this. Experiencing new activities, culture and food, history and nature are excellent. They serve to broaden mental horizons and open the mind to other possibilities. You can also gain insights and new perspectives from reading about the experiences that others have had, both past and present. Books, films, plays and the arts are all in the same area of presenting new perspectives to us.

Our everyday environment affects our mental health too. Spending time with a supportive group of peers or friends who share similar learning interests is game-changing. Living and working in an uncluttered and clean environment, free from unwanted distractions – including your smart devices – are all ways to enhance the quality of our mental life.

Regularly reflecting on the way we think, "meta-cognition", is a good practice. If we continue to think the same thoughts, we only get more of the same. Looking at what works for us and what does not leads to us making informed and desirable changes to our way of thinking and so too our mental life.

Brain health expert Dr Daniel Amen says it well in his book *Change Your Brain, Change Your Life*.[11] No, in case you're wondering, he was not advocating a brain transplant. Instead, he says that by positively changing how our brain operates in terms of its thought patterns, every one of us can positively upgrade our lives. That is in itself an empowering thought right there!

Spiritual Health

"All we have to decide is what to do with the time that is given us."
  – J.R.R. Tolkien, *The Fellowship of the Ring*

We have now come to the fourth and by no means least of the basic human needs. Stephen Covey[9] described it as the "L" referring to legacy. This is useful as a mnemonic for spiritual needs, but we do need to elaborate on what spiritual health is, at least within the general context of personal growth and development. Some among you readers may have a spiritual practice and set of associated beliefs. Some of you have and practise a religious faith. The purpose here in this section is to explore what spiritual health looks like in a very general sense, rather than labelling or promoting specific faith-related practices or beliefs.

In our busy modern lives, we typically follow the daily routine of getting up in the morning, going to work, doing our work, returning from work, and then going to sleep – to be repeated the next day. You could have good health, physically, emotionally and mentally, but do you have the answers to these questions: Where am I going in life? What's the point of doing this? Who am I becoming? Why? I would suggest that being able to come up with satisfying answers to these considerations is, in essence, addressing your spiritual health needs.

To present this in another way, consider you are making a journey by car. The physical integrity of the car pertains to physical health. The sensors and dashboard pertain to emotional health. The in-car navigation and operating system is mental health. The destination of the car and the nature of the journey being made is spiritual health. If the car is not going anywhere in particular, then the journey lacks purpose and direction – there is a lack of spiritual health.

Health in the spiritual sense answers the biggest of questions that we ask: "Why?" We as human beings can be remembered for what we do and the way we do it. But what makes us stand out is the most human of qualities, our Why. We do not need to have a reason to do something, but we can be more engaged in the endeavour when we know why. If we find that we do not know what our why is, then we can create one that suits us! We will go deeper into the topic of purpose later in Chapter 10.

So how can we maintain and enhance our spiritual health? Here are some strategies to explore.

Reflection and Solitude

Spending time regularly in solitude to reflect on yourself and your life, your actions, your important relationships and your work are good ways for you to connect with yourself. Although you will be going through your daily life with yourself, it is easy to lose touch with the inner you, the one beneath your external attributes, your actions and your work. Think of it as spending quality time with yourself so you get to be yourself. This can include journaling, prayer or meditation, if you are so inclined.

Connection and Relationships

Aside from connecting with yourself, you can seek or create better connections and relationships with others. This can be with your significant other, your family members, friends and peers. Looking for common interests or points of agreement will enhance the connection.

Service and Charity

Being of service to others is a great way to enhance your own spiritual well-being. This can include caring for someone in your family or community, mentoring, teaching and doing communal volunteering work. Performing charitable acts can be great for helping others and there is a gift for the giver too.

Practising Acceptance, Gratitude and Forgiveness

It can be easy to pick up and collect what is not beneficial to us in life. This can be in disputes, disagreements, accidents, mishaps, misunderstandings, misaligned acts etc. If we were to keep track of these and not let go, we would be harbouring negativity and resentment – all detrimental to the quality of our lives. What we can do for ourselves is to consciously clean and refresh ourselves. We can do this by letting go. Here is how:

Acceptance. We can accept what has happened or is happening – to deny it is self delusion!

Gratitude. We can intentionally be grateful, even when we may feel negativity, as there can be learning and experience gained.

Forgiveness. We can try to forgive others – and ourselves – for what has happened to us. This is not saying that the other party was right to do whatever they did; rather, it is about detaching ourselves from the emotional and spiritual burden that we have accumulated. Then we can move onwards without carrying all the extra baggage we never chose in the first place.

The practice of acceptance, gratitude and forgiveness can be conducted as a thought exercise of deliberate declarations or, if you practise a faith, as a prayer or affirmation.

I like to think of this as spiritual self care or "spiritual hygiene." It is a bit like cleansing oneself of what we have picked up during the day that is not healthy for our inner selves!

Summary

In this chapter, we first explored the needs we have, as presented in Maslow's hierarchy of needs. We looked at the concept of maintaining balance, including the principle of Yin and Yang. Then we walked through the fundamental human needs represented as physical, emotional, mental and spiritual. We looked at how we can practise self management to ensure that we keep ourselves in optimal health across these dimensions for holistic health. An improvement in one area will contribute positively to health in others.

Having identified how you can better meet the needs that you have, it is down to you to implement the right strategies for you to see results. The key here is to maintain the discipline to lead to meaningful change. By putting strategies that are right for you in place, you will be able to take back control and perform like your better self with a lot less stress. As important as the insights and strategies covered in this chapter on self management are, remember that you do not have to do this alone! Having the support of a coach to work with you can keep you making sustainable progress. You can turn to the Resources section of this book to get more of the support that you need.

In the next chapter, we explore the topic of motivation: what it is and how to remain motivated to make personal growth and change happen.

> *"Self care is not a luxury. It's a discipline."*
>
> – Audre Lorde

Section 2
Starting to Lead

"Success is not final, failure is not fatal: it is the courage to continue that counts."

– Winston Churchill

Chapter 4
Self Motivation

"Keep Going"

*"Early in the morning, when you are reluctant in your laziness
to get up, let this thought be at hand:
'I am rising to do the work of a human being.'"*

– Marcus Aurelius

Starting to Lead

The Self-Motivation Pillar of Personal Mastery

The first three chapters of this book were focused on helping you in "Taking Back Control." We started with raising our awareness and understanding of ourselves and then went to implementing changes to meet our personal needs so that you can start performing well again.

Self Motivation

In the section "Starting To Lead," we will cover the pillars within the Jung Personal Mastery Method that help you to improve your ability to lead yourself to achieve more. This chapter is on the topic of self motivation, our personal drive to achieve.

As the poignant quote from Marcus Aurelius points out, our self motivation enables us to do what we want and need to do. Self motivation enables us to ensure that our personal needs are met. Our level of motivation can be high at times and low at others. Even people perceived as high achievers may have low motivation in certain areas. With good self motivation, we can keep moving forward, even when we may not want to. Self motivation drives us to take sustained action toward our goals and personal development. Without self motivation, we would not progress on anything we start and also not take anything to completion! Without self motivation, we would not be able to meet our needs.

Motivation can be crudely pictured as being influenced by the proverbial "carrot or stick." Wield a stick (figuratively, as I am against animal cruelty) at a donkey, and the animal will likely comply with your demands, if only to avoid being struck. As the experience of pain is not a pleasant one, it acts as a motivator. Conversely, if you were to dangle a carrot in front of the said donkey, you would get the poor beast to comply through the presented idea of being able to eat the proffered snack. Here, pleasure is the motivating factor.

In reality, we all experience motivation related to pain or pleasure. Which would get better results over the short or long term? The immediacy of experiencing pain is perhaps more powerful in motivating us, but no one likes to use pain for their motivation. We are also often, in fact, motivated to move away from pain or the threat of it.

Where Does Motivation Come From?

If you are employed, your employer pays you to do work for them. The monetary reward enables you to pay for the things that you need and want. The motivation originates from an external source; in this case, the paycheck is the "carrot." If you were reprimanded by your boss, the punishment ("stick") would also be a motivator coming from an external source. You are motivated to do a good job to avoid conflict with the boss. These motivations can be extrinsic motivators.

Another type of motivation we have is from within ourselves: intrinsic motivation. In the employee scenario, having intrinsic motivation means you are self-motivated in that you want to do the best you can for your personal growth and learning. You may find motivation in how your work benefits the company's clients or supports your co-workers. You may be motivated by long-term goals, irrespective of what happens in the day-to-day.

It is preferable to have intrinsic motivation because in this way, we are more likely to carry on through despite challenges and difficulties. With intrinsic motivation, we have our motivators that are less affected by our environment, our daily experience or how we feel from one moment to the next. However, in reality, we have a mix of both extrinsic and intrinsic motivation.

In my twenties, I broke a leg during a martial arts training session with friends. The doctor told me the bad news: He estimated that it would take my leg six weeks in plaster to heal – a relatively short time given the clean nature of the break and my physical fitness thanks to my youth. But at that time, six weeks of rest felt like a prison sentence!

My motivation to do anything plummeted to an all-time low. I was used to going out on daily runs and being mobile, not stuck at home. Although the bone fracture healed quickly, the tendons and ligaments took years to recover. I dreamt of running a marathon, and I decided that this was the achievement I would set out to accomplish. After being freed from the plaster cast, despite injury and pain, I did my training interspersed with rest. I was able to complete my first marathon in Paris with a running time of 4.5 hours. The pain in my recovering leg remained with me, but it was worth the achievement.

I later went on to run my second marathon the following year in London – still with challenges from leg pain. My motivation was both extrinsic (to complete a marathon) and intrinsic (I needed to prove to myself I could run again despite the injury I had sustained). Running the marathon as a way to raise money for a disabled children's outdoor activity charity was an additional motivator for me, both extrinsic and intrinsic.

Why We Struggle With Motivation

Knowing what motivates us is one thing. It is another thing entirely to get into action – even when our need is important to us. Why do we struggle at times with motivation? Why do we procrastinate?

A new project or assignment we have can appear to be too large an undertaking. When we feel overwhelmed, we get stuck in a place of inaction. We can get into the rut of overthinking, analysing things like what could go wrong and asking too many "what ifs." Thinking is of little use compared to taking action. It is by taking action that you move forward to a better vantage point than the present one.

As one Chinese proverb goes, "Do not fear moving forward slowly. Fear only to stand still." The hardest step of a journey is to make the first one. Once we make the first one, we have more momentum to help us carry on forward. In the words of Lao Tzu, "A journey of a thousand miles begins with a single step."

Going back to my marathon running, a journey of 26.2 miles (or 42 kilometres) from start to finish can easily feel like a thousand miles instead. While it is helpful to occasionally gauge how far we have travelled or how much further there is to go, it is each step we take that brings us incrementally closer to our goal. The goal of running a marathon is to get to the finish line; the process to get us there is every single step we take to move forward and progress. Trust the process (repeat the single step a sufficient number of times), and you'll achieve the outcome (reach the finish line).

Breaking it down, this is a step-by-step guide we can use:

1. Identify the need or want – the reason for taking action.

2. Identify the goal. Get clear on the precise goal to be reached and the benefit to be gained.

3. Identify the process. Get clear on the steps that will enable you to reach the goal.

4. Implement the process.

5. Reward yourself for the progress made.

Having rewards for progress milestones can be very helpful to sustain motivation – so long as the chosen reward does not threaten to undo the original intended benefits of achieving the overall goal. Imagine how unproductive it would be to have a "blow out" meal to celebrate a milestone in your path to a healthy body weight! The point here is to have a reward that is appropriate and proportionate.

We can observe common fallacies in self motivation in the popular practice of having New Year's Resolutions. I understand that the new year is seen as an opportunity to turn over a new leaf. In my point of view, I stopped doing New Year's resolutions since I strive to improve most days of the year. How many people successfully sustain new habits into the year? Most fall by the wayside before long. Why does this happen?

One factor is that their goals are not broken down into smaller, more manageable milestones. Someone who wants to give up smoking may have more success by staging the reduction of smoking over a pre-planned period, aided by other supportive practices like joining a peer group. For success here, having a defined game plan or strategy is key. That strategy needs to include ways to mitigate the cravings and temptations that will come.

It is important to be clear on why you are enacting a change. The clearer and more compelling the benefits of achieving a goal, the higher the likelihood of success. My dad was able to give up a long-standing smoking habit only after it was pointed out to him that he should be doing it for his grandkids. He managed to give it up completely, and it even took my siblings and me a while to realise he had totally kicked the habit. We celebrate our dad for successfully giving up smoking – it could not have been easy.

I recall the wry observation made by the writer Mark Twain: "Giving up smoking is easy; I have done it hundreds of times." This saying speaks as well of what happens to many well-intended New Year's Resolutions!

Our ability to remain motivated, especially if extrinsically, can fluctuate when we do not feel our best. If we are tired or feeling run down, our motivation level may not be sufficient to achieve our desired goal. We may feel tempted to engage in other lower-priority activities that make us feel better immediately but leave us feeling worse off in the long run. This emphasises the point of how important it is to have good self management practices to maintain our motivation levels at their optimum.

To be successful, especially when it involves making behavioural changes, simply achieving a goal may not be sufficient. What happens after? Do you keep going into more challenging pursuits or revert to old habits? To achieve success in something and keep doing so, we need to do more than tick it off the checklist.

As James Clear in his book *Atomic Habits*[12] points out, our habits affect who we become and who we are determines our habits. For example, to achieve our first marathon and keep being able to complete more feats of endurance, we can think of what successful marathoners do and emulate them. This reminds me of how renowned method actors spend time studying their characters and behaving like them even off the set. It is like assuming the identity of their character so that they can bring more authenticity to their performance.

To complete a marathon, you can "choose" to run a marathon because you want to, or you can run a marathon because you *are* a marathon runner. If you say "I want to run a marathon" and then say "I am a marathon runner", which gives you a stronger sense that you will complete your marathon?

Similarly, a person who wants to lose weight by reducing their calorie intake could choose one of two approaches: either resist any cakes they see or identify as a person who eats healthily. The difference here is that in the first, the person has not changed; they see a cake and are tempted. They need willpower to succeed in resisting the temptation. In the second, the person does not identify as a "cake-eating person," so they would not need much willpower to succeed. It is a bit like a duck that does not push against water resistance but rather glides through it. Why is this distinction important? Simply put, we can create more time for what truly matters by aligning with our successful selves rather than relying on our limited willpower reserves!

Having motivation is like having a force we use to push or pull ourselves along. The stronger the force we have helping us, the better our expected progress is going to be. We will, at times, experience some form of resistance or friction. This resistance acts against our best efforts. Knowing that this resistance is there points to the need to counteract it in some way or reduce it to make it easier for ourselves to push or pull through.

This becomes crucial when we want to get started. When starting something new, we must overcome our natural tendency to remain in a state of inaction. This means letting go of whatever holds us back and removing the barriers that keep us stuck. Essentially, we need to make it easier to move forward rather than stay where we are or do nothing. Someone who wants to start a morning running habit would do well to make sure that their running shoes are in sight and in good condition each morning, have an alarm set at the right time, and have an accountability partner (a running partner or coach) to make sure that they meet their commitment.

Looking at what could be holding you back from following through on your best intentions and then taking steps to remove or reduce them will be helpful for success in your chosen endeavour.

My 9-Step Plan to Improve Self Motivation

1. Identify an area of your life or work that you want to be better motivated for. Be specific and clear on what that is and the benefit you will get from improving it.
2. Reflect on the type of person you could become as you develop motivation in that area. Think of how you would feel differently about yourself and how you would think, communicate and act.
3. Identify a short-term goal to aim for as a milestone achievement.
4. Identify one small, defined, repeatable action that you can take from now on with each day or week.
5. Decide how you want to measure your progress in taking the defined action from step 4. Decide on a small appropriate reward for completing a predetermined number of repeated actions.
6. Identify any potential resistance that could hold you back from making progress and take steps to remove or reduce them.
7. Implement the action each day or week and monitor progress. Remember, consistency is key. If you find yourself slipping, be self-compassionate and continue from where you are.
8. Reflect and celebrate progress made.
9. Seek help from a coach, mentor or peer who can also guide you and act as an accountability partner to strengthen your commitment.

Summary

In this chapter, we explored what self motivation is and the different types. We looked at some reasons why attempts can fail and how we can improve and maintain better self motivation.

Self motivation is essential for achieving, growing and progressing in life. It drives us to fulfil the needs that help us become our best selves. To break free from our comfort zones and improve, we must first gain clarity on why we want to move forward and reach our goals. Success requires a well-thought-out strategy and the consistent implementation of a simple, effective process. Self motivation is key to leadership – leading ourselves first so that we can effectively lead others.

In the next chapter, we will explore an important topic that goes hand-in-hand with self motivation: our resilience – the ability to withstand challenges and adapt to change.

> *"He who has a why to live can bear almost any how."*
>
> – Friedrich Nietzsche

Chapter 5
Resilience
"Ability to Bounce Back and Handle Change"

*"The greatest glory is not in never falling,
but in rising every time we fall."*
– Confucius

Starting to Lead

The Resilience Pillar of Personal Mastery

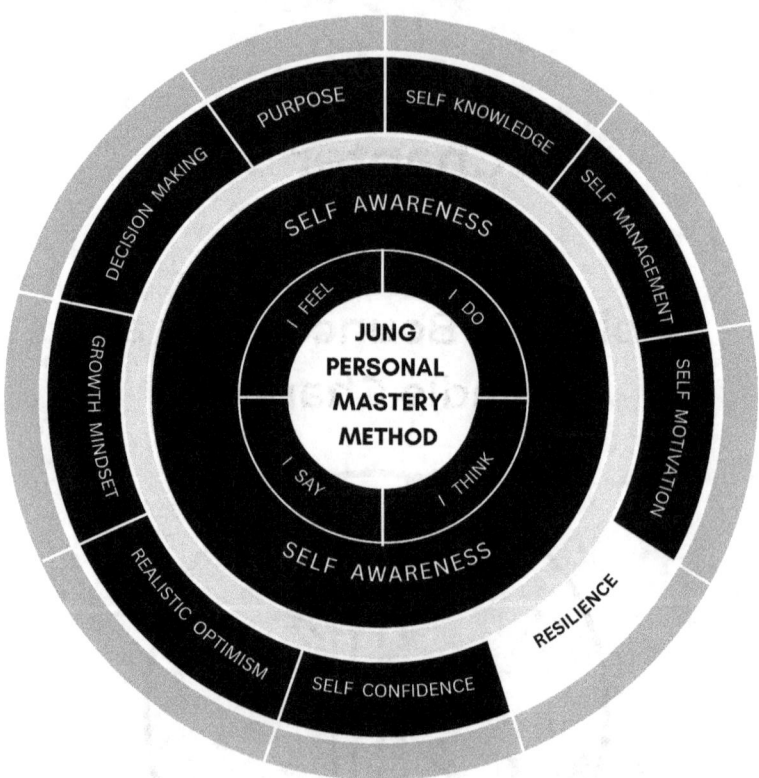

In the last chapter, we explored the big topic of self motivation. It is easy to keep moving when things are going well. It is in the face of challenges and difficulties that we struggle to do so. When faced with adversity, we must dig deep and tap into our inner reserves. To keep going, regardless of whatever hardships are thrown at us, we need the quality of resilience to see us through. In this chapter, we'll explore what it is, why it is important for us in our journeys and how you can develop better resilience.

Challenges beset us all the time. When one challenge is overcome, others take their place. Successes and achievements lead to new challenges. When is life ever "easy"?

There may be times in life when we think things are going well. Inevitably, we begin to see bigger rewards – like recognition at work or more confidence – that we decide to strive towards. Change, too, will present challenges. If you've ever gone through a company reorganisation, then you will know this very well: think of how difficult it was managing all the new responsibilities while staying focused and delivering on your key projects. Motivation can help you keep moving in situations like these, while resilience is what allows you to take the strain and not break under pressure.

What is Resilience?

If you dropped two balls – one made of rubber and the other of glass – from a certain height, you would see the rubber one bounce back off the ground, while the glass one would shatter on impact. The rubber ball can return from the point of impact. Being more resilient like the rubber ball allows you to better withstand the stress and challenges of life. You might be feeling overwhelmed at work, whether due to tight deadlines or a demanding project. These situations draw upon your resilience. The more resilient you are, the higher your ability to handle the pressures you are encountering and keep performing without risking severe fatigue and burnout.

Burnout is defined in the 11th Revision of the International Classification of Diseases (ICD-11) as an occupational phenomenon.[13] It is defined as "a syndrome conceptualized as resulting from chronic workplace stress that has not been successfully managed. It is characterized by three dimensions: feelings of energy depletion or exhaustion; increased mental distance from one's job, or feelings of negativism or cynicism related to one's job; and reduced professional efficacy."

This official definition of burnout is specific to occupational contexts only. Given that the World Health Organisation (WHO) recognises the ICD-11 definition, it supports the development of evidence-based guidelines on mental well-being in the workplace. This expected development by the WHO means that there is a critical need for employers to take steps to promote mental well-being in their employees. This is encouraging and, at the same time, a clarion call for employees to take into account the importance of practising self management consistently and developing improved resilience.

Taking the analogy of the rubber and glass balls, we know that both have innate physical characteristics. Are we not born and stuck with them? Well, if you took the rubber ball and dipped it into liquid nitrogen (which would be at around -196 °C or -320.8°F) and then dropped it, the same ball would break on impact. Now take the other ball and heat it until it becomes a molten globule (at 1,400°C or 2,550°F); the same glass ball would likely have a better chance of remaining in one piece after having been dropped. I am, of course, not suggesting you conduct such experiments physically as they require careful scientific supervision and secure laboratory conditions – this was a thought experiment. The point here is that our natural degree of resilience is not static. We can seek to improve our levels of resilience to better cope and withstand the stresses and challenges that life brings.

Another example of resilience I want to draw upon is bamboo – hence the icon at the beginning of this chapter. In parts of Asia, bamboo is priced for its toughness, strength and ability to flex while maintaining its integrity, even while bearing high levels of physical load. Bamboo is commonly used for scaffolding in building construction, whereas other parts of the world typically rely on steel.

"The bamboo that bends is stronger than the oak that resists."

– Japanese proverb

Types of Resilience

Resilience is not just in the physical sense. It can also mean your emotional, mental and spiritual resilience. There are many ways that resilience in these areas can be developed. What works for one area can also help support the growth of another. Below are the different types, how to start developing them and other ways that may work well for you.

Physical Resilience

Physical resilience means maintaining good health and fitness, which helps reduce the risk of illness and injury. We are also physically resilient when we are well-rested, hydrated and nourished.

Looking after your own physical needs, as explored in Chapter 3, will help to develop this type of resilience. Physical training to improve muscular strength and tone, physical coordination and balance, as well as mobility are all reliable ways to develop physical resilience.

If you are often tired, your ability to withstand stress is diminished, which means that your capacity to function normally will be hampered.

Here are some ways you can focus on developing your physical resilience:

Be physically active. Do strength training, cardiovascular exercises, flexibility training, prioritise regular moderate activity over high-intensity workouts, work with a coach or other professionals as appropriate to support you etc.

Focus on nutrition. Eat balanced meals, ensure adequate hydration and intake of nutrients, vitamins and minerals, include anti-inflammatory foods in your diet such as fatty fish, nuts, turmeric, and reduce intake of sugary foods etc.

Improve your quality of sleep. Adhere to a consistent sleep routine, limit intake of stimulants such as caffeine and screen time before bed, prioritise recovery time, pay attention to how your body is feeling etc.

Emotional Resilience

Emotional resilience can show itself in how we as individuals handle difficult or traumatic emotions. Allowing emotions to be felt and understood is helpful and leads to a better place internally from which to respond appropriately. Having a strong and supportive social network is also important for emotional resilience.

Here are some ways you can focus on developing your emotional resilience:

Cultivate self awareness. Recognise your emotions, identify the triggers for your emotions, and observe your reactions to them.

Develop emotional regulation. Pause before reacting so that you can give yourself a chance to choose how to respond. Practice deep breathing so that you calm your nervous system. Label your emotions so that you can process them and respond more effectively.

Develop empathy. Practice seeing situations from another person's perspective. Strengthen relationships with other people, including those who are important to you. Practice compassion for others who are going through challenging times. Work with a coach or other professional as appropriate to support you.

Mental Resilience

Mental resilience is akin to willpower. You may have heard of the marshmallow test conducted by psychologist Walter Mischel at Stanford in 1970[14] as a study on delayed gratification. In the experiment, children were told that if they resisted eating the marshmallow placed in front of them for 15 minutes – during which they were left alone with the treat by the researcher – they would receive an additional one as a reward.

This and a number of related experiments yielded interesting findings, one of which revealed that focusing on the reward itself increased frustration and made it harder for children to delay gratification. This suggests that thinking too much about the potential reward can actually weaken mental resilience. However, with practice – such as resisting thoughts of the reward or using self distraction – one can improve self control and perform better when faced with temptation.

Here are some ways you can develop your mental resilience:

Cultivate self awareness. Identify triggers that cause stress or discomfort, practice mindfulness exercises, build a support system, nurture relationships with people who are supportive and positive, seek help when you feel that you need it, don't wait for others to ask if you need help, engage in social activities or join groups that promote a sense of belonging, and work with a coach or other professionals as appropriate to support you.

Practice self management. Schedule regular activities that enable you to relax and recuperate, and engage in regular physical exercise.

Continuous learning. Make use of learning opportunities in topics that are of interest to you, whether professionally or personally, as this will give you deeper perspectives that can enrich your ability to handle mentally challenging problems. Seek learning on unfamiliar topics so that you widen your perspective and develop an understanding of context. Some aspects found in diverse fields of interest can be shared.

Spiritual Resilience

Spiritual resilience is holding onto our sense of self, identity, purpose in life, our connection with others and the world around us, and our faith or beliefs.

Here are some ways you can focus on developing your spiritual resilience:

- Clarify your core values and seek ways to live or work more in alignment with them.
- Practice reflection and mindfulness so that you can observe how you live and work.
- Strengthen your support system so that you do not feel alone.

- Embrace gratitude and compassion so that you can develop a healthy perspective on yourself and your relationship with others.
- Volunteer and help others in need so that you can discover the benefits you can provide to others.
- Work with a coach or other professional as appropriate to support you.

In the previous chapter on self motivation, I shared my personal experience of recovering from a broken leg and going on to complete my first marathon. Alongside the lessons learned about my own self motivation, I gained perspectives on personal resilience. There was the ability to recover from a physical injury, with the mental, emotional and spiritual components. There was the mental battle I had during the marathons – especially in my second run when one leg cramped up, likely due to my old injury, from mile 3 (at 4.8 km) all the way to the end of the 26.2-mile (42 km) event!

How did I know with certainty that I had the necessary amount of resilience to pull through and succeed? The honest and simple answer is that I did not. It wasn't until I was subjected to the challenges of the journey that I was able to develop my resilience through a training programme that built up the intensity and duration of running sessions that I could sustain. This improved my resilience from the mental, emotional and spiritual perspectives, apart from the obvious physical one.

My view is that the stories that prove to be the most inspiring and motivating to us are not solely down to how highly motivated the protagonist was (real or imagined), but by how they consistently demonstrated resilience in the face of often small odds of success – whether that be to achieve something grand or simply survive. Someone can be hugely motivated to do something, but if there is little in the way of resistance or challenge, then the achievement becomes relatively easy and of less significance. A story of a person overcoming adversity, risking all, and yet prevails, is a story we are all drawn to. Why? I think that such stories show us something about the power of being human, the power of the human spirit that can push us to perform awe-inspiring feats despite acknowledged limitations.

Hero of Resilience: Nelson Mandela

The story of Nelson Mandela's life is one such story, recounted in his own words in the autobiography *Long Walk to Freedom*.[15] In South Africa, having witnessed the stark injustices of apartheid from an early age, he became involved in activism. His commitment to this cause came at a high personal cost: He spent 27 years in prison, many of which were on Robben Island, enduring harsh conditions as well as separation from family. Even under hardship in prison, Mandela showed incredible personal leadership. He continued to demonstrate dignity, resilience and commitment to his chosen cause. He inspired hope in fellow prisoners and treated his captors with respect. He inspired people worldwide. Enduring hardship and facing obstacles over decades, Mandela emerged from prison with continued resilience to assume the role of President of South Africa and reform the nation. All this while showing forgiveness and grace to those who held him captive. If this is not an awe-inspiring story of a person's resilience, then I do not know what is.

> *"I can be changed by what happens to me.*
> *But I refuse to allow it to reduce me."*
>
> – Maya Angelou

The importance of time spent training in intentional practice matters. It builds up your own experience while adding to resilience. Some fighting arts like boxing do involve getting "used" to being hit. In life and work, we are always subject to the risk of "getting hit," not in a literal way, but by the challenges that present themselves. We can find ourselves gaining experience and developing resilience from these moments.

We can also gain more resilience by choosing to do things that lie slightly outside our usual zone of ability and comfort. At work, this can take the form of co-leading a big project as a next opportunity for growth instead of taking a full leadership role for a smaller project. We can adopt resilience-enforcing habits to improve too. Developing greater resilience enables you to withstand more stresses and strains and take on challenges with better capability.

Being aware of where your current limitations lie is just as important as deciding to improve your resilience in a certain area. A little challenge just outside your current comfort zone is good for growth and resilience-building. Too much challenge in one dose can prove damaging. From a state of awareness of your current limitations, you can make better decisions as you establish and adhere to your boundaries.

Another point to bear in mind is that you must be clear and specific on the nature of resilience you want to develop. This allows you to effectively measure progress and the benefits derived therewith.

Resilience is also our ability to handle change. While we would prefer for things to remain the same and comfortable, the reality is that we live in a world where change is a permanent feature – including within ourselves. Everything is in flux. To survive, and even better, to thrive, we need to be adaptable, to flex with stresses and strains that come from change.

An example of this can be taken from building design. In earthquake-prone areas of the world, the most earthquake-resistant buildings are designed with flexible structures that can move and adapt to external forces, reducing the risk of collapse while maintaining structural integrity. In contrast, buildings that are overly rigid and stiff are more prone to damage. This demonstrates that resilience is best achieved by combining strength with flexibility.

Our ability to be resilient is also dependent on our habits and systems of self management. The better our state physically, emotionally, mentally and spiritually, the more fully we can bring ourselves to play and have good levels of resilience.

Summary

Resilience is a characteristic that helps us withstand the challenges that life brings us and enables us to live more fully. It enables us to handle stress and change. It enables us to adapt.

The great thing about resilience is that it can be trained and developed; you do not have to rely on what you innately have. Gaining resilience does not happen with quick fixes. Like many things, it takes time, intentional practice and learning to attain. Practicing through doing is key here. Improvements to resilience can arise from other components of personal mastery covered in this book. Growth in one type of resilience can enhance growth in others. Motivation is a contributing factor, as is the capacity for good self management. There are others, too, that we shall uncover in due course.

I encourage you to look at your current level of resilience and start getting practical, relevant experiences to improve. You will then be better prepared to take on challenges, both current and future. Having someone to help you can boost your resilience levels, especially in terms of a coach who is tasked to help you succeed. Resilience fuels self motivation, enabling you to achieve and perform more sustainably. It also helps you trust in your abilities and judgment. In the next chapter, we will explore this further as we delve into the crucial topic of self confidence – the foundation for "Starting to Lead."

> *"You, me, or nobody is gonna hit as hard as life. But it ain't about how hard you hit. It's about how hard you can get hit and keep moving forward. That's how winning is done!"*
>
> – Sylvester Stallone, *Rocky Balboa*

Chapter 6
Self Confidence
"Trust Your Judgement and Ability"

"Always be yourself, express yourself, have faith in yourself, do not go out and look for a successful personality and duplicate it."
– Bruce Lee

Starting to Lead

The Self-Confidence Pillar of Personal Mastery

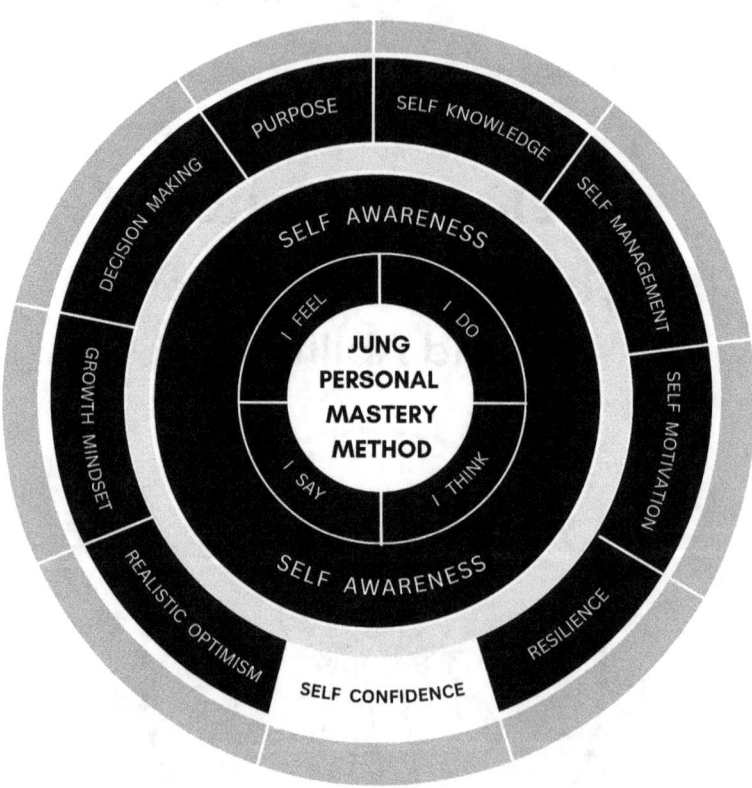

We have covered the topics of self motivation and resilience, which are both key pillars of personal mastery for you "Starting To Lead." Another essential component of leading is self confidence, which comes down to trusting in your judgement and ability.

If you ask people what they wish they had more of, many would likely say they'd wish for more confidence. You may have seen some people in the media or your own circles who appear to be on another level of self confidence. They're more than capable of public speaking, speaking up in debates, asking questions in an open forum, learning and developing new skills or leading a team.

We all have a notion of what self confidence is, but what is it exactly? And more importantly for us, is it something we can develop more of and if so, how? In this chapter, we will explore these points.

What is Self Confidence?

Confidence is defined as the feeling of belief or trust that a person or thing is reliable. Self confidence is the trust in oneself so that one can accomplish what one wants to in the future. An interesting distinction is that self confidence is not to be confused with self esteem, which relates to one's evaluation of their own worth. People with self confidence are generally able to perform well, so they trust in themselves to apply themselves to the task, project or challenge.

Self confidence has been a frequent topic throughout history, literature and thought. I'll pick out some examples to illustrate:

Moses, Bible, Exodus 3-4

In the story entitled "Moses and the Burning Bush," Moses encounters God for the first time and is instructed to speak to the Pharaoh and lead the Israelites out of Egypt. Moses is reluctant, expressing a lack of self confidence. At one point, he protests to God, saying, "O Lord, I have never been eloquent, neither in the past nor since you have spoken to your servant. I am slow of speech and tongue." Yet the Moses we know prevailed with some help and prompting from God to become the leader of the Israelites.

Confucius, 551-479 BCE

The philosopher Confucius lived during a time of great social and political upheaval known in China as the Spring and Autumn period. He believed that society could improve through moral behaviour, virtue and proper conduct. Education and virtue were held by him to be transformative, even when rulers at the time were more interested in military power and domination. Despite the challenges, he travelled between states, advising rulers of his ideas and implementation strategies, which were often ignored. His criticisms of some rulers for their moral conduct were also dismissed. Despite having been largely ignored in his time, Confucius showed self confidence by continuing to champion his ideas – today, he is one of the most admired thinkers of history. As he once said, "It does not matter how slowly you go as long as you do not stop."

Leonardo da Vinci, 1452-1519

Leonardo da Vinci grew up without a conventional academic upbringing, yet he was confident in his ability to master multiple disciplines. In a letter to the Duke of Milan, Ludovico il Moro Sforza, for patronage, da Vinci spoke of how he could provide services by developing military technology. At the end of that same letter, he added as an afterthought that he could also paint. This was the renowned painter of the *Mona Lisa* and *The Last Supper*, among many world-famous pieces of art!

What About Your Self Confidence?

At this point, you may be thinking, "All clear from those examples, but how does having self confidence relate to me?" What this thinking points to is the level of self belief one has! If today you are able to walk on your own two feet, that only means there was once a time you went through many trials and errors in order to do so. Think back to yourself as a toddler, falling down repeatedly before your arms and legs finally developed enough strength to push you up from the ground and walk. It may have hurt at times, but you kept on trying until you became more coordinated and balanced – eventually being able to walk with competence.

This increased competence is what gave you more confidence in your walking ability. The more evidence you create of your improving competence, the better your self confidence. Interestingly, in your journey to become a walking human being, you persisted and did not give up trying!

I had to relearn how to walk after recovering from my broken leg. It took me a while to be able to walk and run again and even regain the confidence from competence.

I regularly do public speaking, whether at staged events or at my local church. I developed confidence through practice and doing. Notice, however, that despite a good level of confidence (in my opinion) in public speaking, I have at times found it uncomfortable to call someone I do not know by phone. I would also feel a lack of confidence if I were to sing in front of the same audience I regularly speak to!

What makes having more self confidence so challenging? One key factor is rooted in fear. That fear can take a number of nuances, which we'll explore below.

Fear of Failure

Failure is not as attractive to us as success. Our egos generally dislike it. Social media posts highlight successes more than failures. Talking openly about failures takes a lot of humility and can feel shameful at times. Experiencing failure hurts the ego. But speak to the successful and you'll notice many went through a string of failures before reaching a degree of success. Success is often seen as a highlight rather than an accurate reflection of our daily experiences – though this depends on how we choose to define success.

If we do not try something new or use an alternative, unfamiliar approach, we reduce our failure rate! But this is a guaranteed way to get stuck and not grow our skills and abilities. Despite our attempts to overcome our fear of failure, the fear may remain. It is key to review our failures on the way and use the feedback to make intentional adjustments for improved success rate.

Fear of Being "Found Out" (Imposter Syndrome)

A common fear we experience when stepping into unfamiliar environments, like a new role at work or an entirely new industry, is the inner critic thinking we should not be there. Our perception of our skills, experiences and identity disqualifies our plausibility for being there and enhances our fear of being found out.

This is often labelled as "imposter syndrome," which I find to be a misleading term. This term is from a 1978 published study paper entitled "The imposter phenomenon in high achieving women: Dynamics and therapeutic intervention" by psychologists Pauline Clance and Suzanne Imes.[16] The described self doubt is understood to be quite normal and prevalent in normal functional individuals rather than as a mental impairment implied by the use of the word "syndrome." Arriving at a place of self awareness and acceptance of this phenomenon is helpful to grow from this feeling of self doubt.

Fear of Judgement and Rejection

By nature, we human beings are tribal creatures. We have an innate need to be accepted and included. We want to "fit in." However, this desire can sometimes lead people to adopt an alternate identity to gain acceptance, at the cost of their authenticity. We thrive on connections with other people and our communities, especially those with whom we share values and perspectives. When doing something uniquely new or unconventional, we risk judgment and rejection from others. In times past, such judgement and rejection could have life-changing consequences such as our ability to survive or our proximity to important resources like shelter, safety, food and water.

We have not lost that unconscious fear of judgement and rejection to this day. The judgement from others is one thing, but we are also prone to judgement from ourselves, which can prove to be a powerful force that holds us back to keep us safe. This safety from doing anything new, to keep us safe from judgement and rejection, comes with a price: not being able to get past the fear and grow in our self confidence.

Getting past this involves self awareness and acceptance before doing what the fear is keeping you from doing. You could say that fear is pulling you in the opposite direction of where you need to go.

We have explored three aspects where fear makes it challenging for us to be more self confident. It is important to note that it is what it is – perfectly normal. Also we can employ strategies to develop better self confidence.

Another useful perspective to offer here is to look at the word FEAR as an acronym for False Evidence Appearing Real. Our perception of the future – the unknown – can be easily skewed and biased by how we feel about it. Reminding ourselves of this acronym can help to reset our perspective and perception so that we can envision more positive and useful outcomes from taking action regardless. It is taking action despite fear, being braver, that moves us forward, to reduce overthinking and procrastinating. A point to add is that we can choose our attitude, adopting one geared towards success through taking action even while gripped by fear. The only failure we should find difficult to accept is that from not trying!

> *"Believe you can and you're halfway there."*
> – Theodore Roosevelt

Earlier in this book, I recounted a vivid personal experience when I was laughed at by the company CEO and 2,000 on-site employees at a company meeting. Posing a genuine question in a public setting to the CEO took bravery (I know!). Responding with a clear answer and follow-up question took courage too, especially with the perception that I could get fired on the spot by the CEO. A fellow coach called Rob McPhilips described this event as my "one shot," referencing Eminem from the film *8 Mile* in his "The Unified Team" podcast interview with me – everything in that moment came down to taking that one critical shot at the risk of losing everything.

"How did I do that?" I ask myself. In truth, I do not know how; I just did what I had to do to survive in the moment or risk crumbling on the spot! I had to do something. What is insightful for me is what I gained from this pivotal experience. It strengthened my self confidence and gave me a personally lived story I could take forward and share with my coaching clients (and you, my reader) to help them grow in self confidence.

How to Improve Self Confidence

Fear is a familiar feature of our daily existence, especially when we do things that are different and new. With this feeling of fear comes negative thoughts that enter our minds uninvited. Psychiatrist and brain disorder specialist Dr. Daniel Amen came up with a term in the 1990s to describe them: Automatic Negative Thoughts (ANTs).[17] He decided on the acronym after returning home from a long, hard day seeing patients at the clinic only to see that his kitchen was overrun with ants. His insight was that the negative thoughts of his patients were like the errant ants in the kitchen, taking away happiness from any moment.

When we pay too much attention to these ANTs, our self confidence is lowered. The good news is that we can learn to handle these thoughts effectively through a process that Dr. Amen called "Killing ANTs." I'll share one technique here.

One simple way to develop self confidence by "Killing ANTs" is called the ABRA technique, introduced by memory expert Jim Kwik.[18] The acronym stands for:

    A – Acknowledge

    B – Breathe

    R – Release

    A – Align

To practise this technique, make sure you are seated comfortably in a calm and safe space, and that you are not engaged in any another activity that requires your attention. You may choose to close your eyes during the exercise.

Acknowledge. Acknowledge the negative thought that has come to you.

Breathe. Breathe in deeply and slowly through your nose into your abdomen and out through your mouth. This will help you to relax and focus.

Release. Release the negative thought, imagining the thought leaving your body as you breathe out through your mouth.

Align. Align yourself back to the truth about who you are. Say a positive affirmation about yourself. This affirmation can be directly opposite to the negative thought that entered your mind originally.

Repeat the ABRA technique each time you become aware of ANTs that enter your mind and whenever you can spare a couple of minutes to do so.

Apply this technique in small steps. You may decide to try this once a day at first, before you feel comfortable with using it throughout the day as needed. My hope is that the application of this technique helps you to develop your self confidence to achieve what you want while remaining true to yourself.

Summary

Self confidence is the trust one has in their judgement and abilities. Rather than a trait we are born with, it is an aptitude that we can grow and develop. With more self confidence, we can attempt more challenging projects and tasks or acquire and strengthen skills – all achieved despite the fears we may feel. It is the fears that are largely responsible for holding us back by lowering self confidence. However, we can learn to handle the fears and ANTs to move forward and grow. It is hoped that the application of the technique, along with self awareness and self management can support the growth of your self confidence.

With self confidence, you have a sense of self belief and trust in your abilities and experience. Coupled with self motivation and resilience, you will have developed the aptitude of "Starting To Lead" yourself and others. In the next section of this book, we will explore how to uplevel your ability to lead so that you can win more in life and work. This all involves developing your mindset a stage further!

> "Because one believes in oneself, one doesn't try to convince.
> Because one is content with oneself, one doesn't need the other's approval.
> Because one accepts oneself, the whole world accepts him or her."
>
> – Lao Tzu

Section 3
Winning More

"Success is a journey, not a destination."

– Bruce Lee

Section 3
Whitmore

Chapter 7
Realistic Optimism
"Seeing Opportunities for Taking Positive Action"

"The pessimist complains about the wind; the optimist expects it to change; the realist adjusts the sails."
– William Arthur Ward

Winning More

The Realistic Optimism Pillar of Personal Mastery

We have just explored the great topic of self confidence, its importance and how to develop it further. It is a great thing to recognise this is a characteristic each one of us can improve on. Furthermore, it is a feeling that we can choose to have regardless of the fear we are experiencing. Self confidence is a crucial skill to have to start to lead yourself and others.

Realistic Optimism

This next section is called "Winning More" and will have three chapters, starting with Realistic Optimism. We shall discover three new pillars to further upgrade our mindset so that we can be more successful.

So here's a question for you right now: "How are you?" How do you typically respond to this question? How do other people normally reply? There are generally three types of answers: neutral responses like "I'm fine" or "Not too bad"; positive ones such as "Great!" or "Good!"; and negative replies like "Not great" or "Don't ask." A person may be confident, but what they reply to a question like "How are you?" can say something about the way they perceive the world and themselves. In turn, this perception influences how they behave, whether or not their reply reflects their true feelings.

Imagine yourself having a drink at a bar with friends when the discussion turns to a contemplation of the meaning of life. Someone may then ask, "Is the glass half full or half empty?" As usual, this little thought exercise is aimed at finding out who is an optimist and who is a pessimist, with the former seeing it as "half full" and the latter as "half empty." In my point of view, this contemplative exercise is limited – whether you view that glass as an optimist or pessimist, nothing about the glass and its contents changes.

Instead, I like to think of the poem by William Arthur Ward quoted at the start of this chapter. The pessimist sees only the negative side of the situation. In their minds, no matter how stable or positive a situation is, there can only be a bleak outcome. The optimist, on the other hand, sees the positive side and relies on hope to get themselves through. However, both the pessimist and the optimist are mere passive bystanders to what is happening around them; it is as if they are simply passengers.

Hope alone is not a reliable strategy! In the poem, there is the realist – not to be confused with pessimists who claim to be realists but take no action – whom I call the realistic optimist. This person has hope *and* readily takes action to navigate their way through life's challenges. The realistic optimist has effectively taken the "driver's seat" or become the "captain" in this illustration. The realistic optimist recognises that the wind is not within their control, so they apply control over what they can, not just in terms of what is physically around them but also their being or state (mental, physical, emotional and spiritual).

The term "realistic optimism" originated from the 2001 American Psychologist article, "In search of realistic optimism: Meaning, knowledge, and warm fuzziness" by psychologist Sandra L. Schneider[19]. This idea of the realistic optimist reminds me of the final lines of the poem *Invictus* by William Ernest Henley: "I am the master of my fate, I am the captain of my soul."

I have seen job advertisements that, aside from listing technical requirements, state the need for a "can do" attitude. They are looking for someone who is solution- and task-orientated, a person who likes to take on challenges. This can be considered the opposite attitude of only focusing (and potentially ruminating) on problems.

I recall a former manager of mine saying, "Come to me with solutions, not problems!" It took me some time to understand what he meant and act accordingly. Having a mindset of realistic optimism is just the ticket to thriving in the face of change and challenges!

One of the most powerful messages for me is often attributed to Viktor Frankl (or Stephen R. Covey): "Between stimulus and response, there is a space. In that space is our power to choose our response. In our response lies our growth and our freedom." The "space" described may not be readily apparent to us, especially when we find ourselves in difficult and challenging circumstances.

By choosing to become aware of the opportunities that present themselves, we become available to take the chance to act. I think that this is central to realistic optimism. It is the self-propelled mindset that initiates taking meaningful or strategic action. Often, we find ourselves just reacting to what is happening, but with increased awareness and intentioned practice, we develop better "muscles" to choose our responses.

Realising that we have the capacity to decide how we respond is powerful, yet it can be hard to grasp as a concept. Through martial arts, I'm learning this firsthand. When training in hand-to-hand combat, I practice staying aware of my partner's attacks and responding with defense and counters. Earlier in my training journey, I would instinctively react – and sometimes panic – whenever I was "attacked," but over time, I've improved.

This has shown me that we can all get better at adapting, becoming realistic optimists in the process. I believe you can too!

Hero of Realistic Optimism: Jack Ma

There are many well-known people who have achieved success, in part, by embracing optimism through action despite constant challenges.

One such person is Jack Ma, a Chinese business magnate, investor and philanthropist. As of February 2024, Ma was named the seventh wealthiest person in China and the 45th wealthiest person in the world, as ranked by the Bloomberg Billionaires Index. Ma faced numerous rejections early on in life – including ten unsuccessful applications to Harvard Business School. He applied for entry-level jobs at over 30 places, including fast food restaurants, and was rejected by all. Beyond resilience, Ma embodied realistic optimism. He learned from his experiences and persistently moved forward. Many people in his situation may have decided to give up altogether! Ma remained optimistic but cautious and took positive action at each step of the way.

Among many achievements, Ma went on to create the hugely successful e-commerce platform, Alibaba.

How to Develop Realistic Optimism

You now hopefully have a firm grasp of what realistic optimism is. But how can you develop it? What if you do not identify as being optimistic at all? It takes time and practice to grow in this, as is usual with many things. It starts with an intention to change positively. That is in itself an expression of realistic optimism!

Here is my 4A's framework to mastering realistic optimism:

The 4A's Framework To Mastering Realistic Optimism

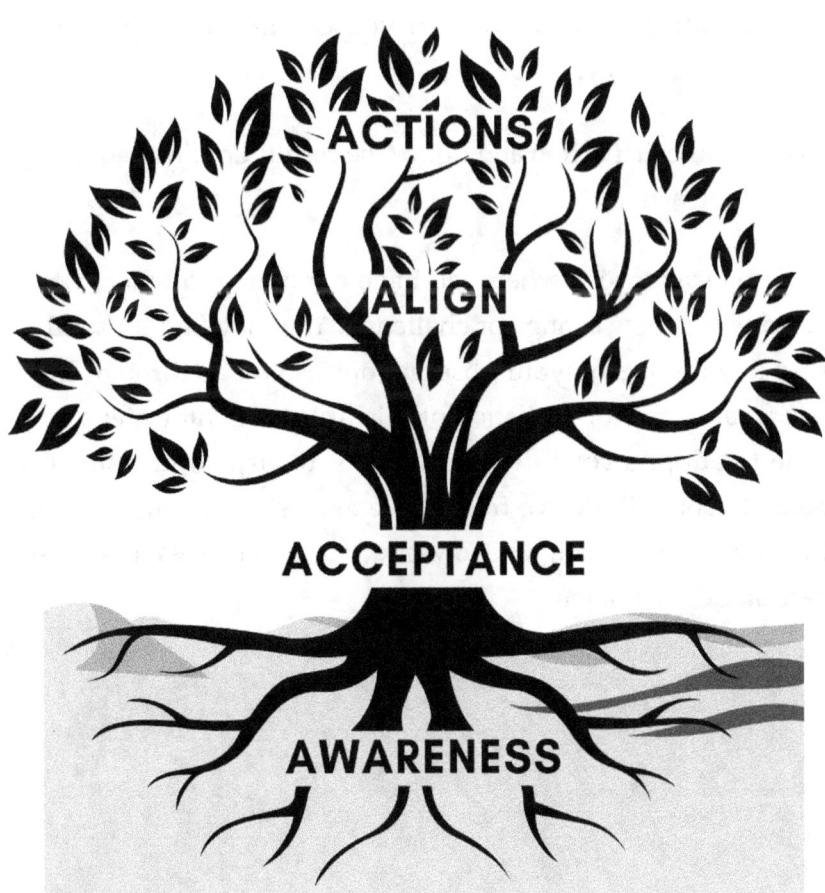

Awareness. Notice the nature of the change or challenge. Notice what is happening around you, how you are feeling and thinking, how others are behaving.

Acceptance. Accept reality as it is, and focus on taking action where you have control. Accept that there are also things outside your control.

Align. Shift your focus to what you can do to progress from where you are now.

Action. Take that action and notice the result! Continue adjusting and taking action.

Use this framework when you have a moment to reflect when faced with a new change or challenge. You may find it useful to take down notes on your observations as you go through the 4 A's framework for realistic optimism. It takes little steps over time to adopt a consistent mindset of realistic optimism. The benefits you will derive from it are extensive in your personal life, the approach you take to work and career, as well as in self care and development!

Summary

In this chapter, we explored the mindset identified as "realistic optimism" and how it is distinct from pessimism and pure optimism. Realistic optimism is firmly grounded in a positive mindset that focuses on opportunities for positive action. It is a mindset of proactive leadership to navigate through change and the unknown. The implications this has to one's own personal life, work and career are wide-ranging, bringing great benefits to the way we can approach life.

Choosing a positive mindset is a powerful first step toward becoming a realistic optimist. The mindset of a realistic optimist is self enhancing. In the next chapter, we will explore another mindset that can enhance the mindset of the realistic optimist even more so they can keep winning in life and work! This, as we will discover, is about seeking opportunities to learn and apply.

"You must never confuse faith that you will prevail in the end – which you can never afford to lose – with the discipline to confront the most brutal facts of your current reality, whatever they might be."

– Jim Stockdale

Chapter 8
Growth Mindset
"Continuous Learning and Application"

"You're in charge of your mind. You can help it grow by using it in the right way."
– Carol Dweck

Winning More

The Growth Mindset Pillar of Personal Mastery

In the last chapter, we explored realistic optimism – a mindset that blends a positive outlook with action – which is not only beneficial but essential in our personal lives, work, and careers. Taking the theme of positive mindsets further, we now venture into the topic of the growth mindset. We will uncover what it is, the critical importance it has for each and every one of us and how to cultivate it for ourselves.

What is a Growth Mindset?

For this exploration, I will work under the assumption that you may not understand fully what a growth mindset is. The terms "fixed mindset" and "growth mindset" were coined by Dr. Carol Dweck, professor of psychology at Stanford University, in her 2006 book *Mindset: The New Psychology of Success*.[20] They pertain to the beliefs people have about their circumstances and abilities and how they choose to act.

Dr. Dweck observed from her earlier studies of children's behaviour in the 1970s that some were more willing to take on challenges than others. Another notable observation she made is that some children were able to recover from setbacks and failures, while others were devastated by them. Dr. Dweck went on to study how the belief people have in their ability and intelligence affected performance in occupational success and in interpersonal relationships. Individuals who readily took on challenges and recovered from setbacks were said by Dr. Dweck to demonstrate having a "growth mindset." Those who did not were said to have a more "fixed mindset."

A Fixed Mindset and a Growth Mindset

To better understand these two types, let us consider an analogy. Imagine you are choosing between two different types of bank accounts into which you can put your financial savings. One (A) is a "fixed" account that keeps your financial savings safe, and after 12 months, you can retrieve the exact same amount of money as what you put in earlier – there was 0% growth. The other (B) option open to you is a "growth" account that pays 5% over time so that after 12 months, you will have 5% more money. Which account do you choose to place your savings in?

I would safely guess that most of you would opt for account B, the one that pays you 5% interest so that you have growth in your savings. Why would you want a growth account above a fixed account? Well, simply put, you could do more with an increased amount of money in savings than no increase, assuming you choose to use it for a purchase or investment.

Taking this illustration further with another analogy, let's say you are presented with two similar job opportunities. Job A offers you 12 months of employment with no increased salary or any new opportunities at the end of it. Job B offers you a promised increased salary and new promotion opportunities at the end of the 12 months. All things being equal, which job do you go for? Job A or Job B?

I think you will choose the second because it offers you growth via improved salary and new opportunities at the end of the contract.

Most people want growth in their lives in some form, be it personal or professional, although not everyone acts according to what they want in this regard. We may also differ in terms of the rate of growth that we are comfortable with. Growth rats can also be perceived as a risk. For Job B, with promised growth, there is an implication that you may have to work harder and do things you are not used to, especially if there are new job opportunities at the end of it!

Constant growth is generally better than being "fixed," and this applies to our mindset. A fixed mindset is closed, unchanging and not open to learning. It is akin to always thinking and acting the same way, leading to the same results and no growth. A growth mindset, on the other hand, is open, adaptable and engaged in continuous learning.

Comparison of Fixed and Growth Mindsets

Fixed Mindset	Growth Mindset
Closed to change and new things	Open to change and new things
Avoids challenges	Faces challenges
Believes talents and intelligence are innate gifts and unchanging efforts are focused on self validation not open to learning	Believes talent and intelligence can be developed through • hard effort • good strategy • accepting input from others • putting energy into learning
Focused on the past	Focused on the future
Competition	Collaboration

A person with a more fixed mindset believes that their talent and intelligence cannot be developed. They are focused on past achievements and less receptive to new learning and experiences. They are resistant to change and new challenges. They are constantly competing with others, focusing on performance rather than actual growth.

On the other hand, the individual who has a growth mindset believes their talent and intelligence can be improved. The fact that you, my reader, are here proves that you already have some level of a growth mindset. Wanting to develop one is characteristic of a growth mindset in itself. A person with a growth mindset is forward-focused and believes in hard effort, the application of good strategy and learning. They lean towards being collaborative in order to grow and develop. They typically face the unknown and the world of change and challenges head-on. They view change and challenges as opportunities to learn and grow. For them, failures are important events that provide valuable feedback as well as successes. They achieve goals that exceed prior expectations. They are individuals who want to learn and grow continually. They apply what they learned (for example, from this book) and test themselves. They are more likely to seek support from coaches and mentors. They are also more likely to help others to develop too. In fact, the concept of coaching, speaking as a coach and mentor myself, is grounded in the principle of encouraging a growth mindset in the clients that coaches work with.

A phrase that comes to mind is one that Bruce Lee said: "Empty your cup." If one's mind is focused only on what one knows, then what space remains to take on what is new? There is a saying in martial arts training about adopting the "beginner's mind" or "the white belt mentality" – no matter how experienced or adept one is, it is important to think like a beginner in order to keep learning!

A person with a growth mindset is likely to achieve more and continually develop skills and intelligence. Look at athletes who compete. They are all at the top of their game, yet they all have coaches and trainers. It is the same with top company executives and leaders. This is because they recognise that coaches and trainers can push and encourage them to keep improving and performing at their best.

In your work, you might lead a team to advance their projects, support their growth, help them perform at their best, and prepare them to become future leaders – all of which align with a growth-oriented mindset. On the other hand, if you withhold opportunities for learning and development or prevent your team from taking on challenging projects, you may be operating with a more fixed mindset.

I recall my first few times riding a glider. In case you did not know, a glider is a light aircraft that has no active means of propulsion – no engine or motor – apart from an initial winch cable at launch. Once in the air, the glider rides the air currents and rising warm air.

On my second series of flights, my experienced pilot gave me the chance to take full control of the glider for a few moments while in flight. It was an exciting opportunity; a little scary because it was my first time and thrilling as well. I tried taking in what my instincts were telling me and was doing the best I could to understand what was happening to the aircraft in response to my efforts to manoeuvre. I had thought earlier that it should be fairly easy in theory, but practical experience proved that to be untrue! I was determined to get better and applied myself in the next flight.

At the very least, I gained a clearer sense of what "better" looked and felt like. I was clearly outside my comfort zone – you could say I was in my growth zone. To me, this was proof of a growth mindset in action. With a more fixed mindset, I might have given up or never even allowed myself to try.

Applying the Growth Mindset

When you take a moment to think about your life or your work, you will notice that you encounter problems or challenges. There will be situations you are in that are difficult for you and others around you. The mindset with which you perceive these situations determines your experience of them and your approach to resolving them. When you experience failure, is your natural tendency to view it as a terrible outcome or do you seek to find a positive learning from it? Conversely, when you achieve or succeed, is your tendency to brush it off as mere luck or do you try to understand what you did that worked well and what you could do differently to improve your outcome further? Who else was involved in helping you achieve the outcome under consideration?

Growth Mindset

In Chapter 7, we discovered the benefit of a realistic, optimistic mindset. This mindset, as you may have already surmised, is a growth mindset. The other mindsets pertinent to the pessimist or the optimist are indicative of fixed mindsets. Seeking to think differently about a situation or to do something differently in order to move on is a hallmark of a growth mindset.

Imagine that you are faced with a big organisational change in the company you work for. You are dreading this as it means a lot of uncertainty and hard decisions to be made, perhaps involving your role in cutting down the size of your workforce. You could decide to act only as the messenger and simply communicate the decision made by senior leadership without taking action to ensure that your workforce members' interests are taken into consideration. This would be indicative of a fixed mindset. Alternatively, you could decide to consult with your employees and determine how best to represent their interests to senior leadership, such that your workforce feels valued and still receives opportunities to grow and move forward. This alternative approach is not easy by any means, but it is reflective of a growth mindset. A growth mindset is focused on opportunities, even with challenges present.

Consider another scenario wherein your company's senior management appoints you to lead a new project. The project's output will have far-reaching implications for the company. It would involve you working differently from how you have done so previously in your company role. Do you accept or reject it? If you reject it because you think it would just be a source of more work and more stress, you may be acting from a fixed mindset. If you decide to find out more and consult with senior management before making a more considered decision, you would be behaving with a more growth-oriented mindset. Which is better? I would encourage you to consider that a growth mindset is better for you than a fixed mindset, however, you do need to understand which is better for you.

Where do you see yourself with your current mindset? Do you perceive yourself as having more of a growth or fixed mindset? In what area of your life or work do you notice your mindset is one way or the other?

Many of the clients I work with want to improve their self confidence so that they can become more effective communicators at work or be more prepared to make difficult decisions. A key component of the coaching process that I take them through involves enhancing their growth mindset while diminishing their existing tendencies to adopt a fixed mindset. This invariably starts with developing the foundations of self awareness in the individual. Working with a coach can be a powerful way to develop a more robust growth mindset.

Another observation we can make about ourselves and others is the extent to which we are creative, collaborative, or both. When have you noticed this? Both of these aptitudes point to a growth mindset. Conversely, think of when we are not creative or collaborative; how does this help us? These instances indicate a fixed mindset perspective.

It is easy to fall into the trap of negatively judging oneself or others for having a fixed mindset. In fact, the act of negatively judging is pertinent to a fixed mindset. Instead, it is helpful to notice the mindset in ourselves and others without judgment. Noticing followed by acceptance is a good way to move forward. We are where we are. Knowing this enables us to decide what to do next to move forward and improve. This thought process is in itself part of a growth mindset.

A Hero of the Growth Mindset: Helen Keller

A hero of the growth mindset for me is Helen Keller. She was an extraordinary American author and educator who was blind and deaf. In early life, she learned to feel objects and associate their names as spelt out on her palm. She learned to read by feeling raised words on cardboard. Her learning feats were amazing and she learned to speak and even lipread by feeling the lips and throat of the speaker.

Her work included co-founding the American Civil Liberties Union with American civil rights activist Roger Nash Baldwin in 1920. She also championed efforts to improve the treatment of the deaf and the blind. She authored a number of books, including *Optimism* (1903) and *Light in My Darkness* (1927).

How to Improve Your Growth Mindset

In our exploration of the benefits of the growth mindset as compared to the fixed mindset so far, you may now be aware of evidence of a growth mindset or fixed mindset in your approach to professional and personal life. Here is how you can start to develop a better growth mindset using my 4 A's framework.

The 4A's Framework To Mastering A Growth Mindset

Awareness. Start by being aware of key aspects of your professional and personal life. Notice where you tend to have a growth mindset and where you tend to have a fixed mindset.

Acceptance. It is important to accept your current level of growth mindset and fixed mindset. I add here that it is perfectly acceptable to have a fixed mindset in areas of your life, as long as you notice the opportunity to do something positive with it in due course.

Align. In a key area of your personal or professional life, what is a small practical change you could make that is aligned with the growth mindset?

Action. Take that action, notice the results and apply adjustments. If necessary, seek support from a coach.

One aspect of the growth mindset I would like to emphasise here is that application is key to growth. I could, for example, have amassed a great academic understanding of a skill, but it would be of limited value if I did not actively use it. Think of how you learned how to drive a car. You learn what you need most effectively from doing and from gaining practical experience. A growth mindset is an active mindset, grounded in action.

Summary

Developing a growth mindset is invaluable to all. It enables people to continually learn, develop and become more skilled and experienced. The benefits of this mindset help enhance learning and other qualities like confidence and resilience. It enables people to face change and the unknown. It enables people to view problems and failures as challenges and opportunities to learn from and improve.

The beauty of the growth mindset is that it is available to all who choose to claim and grow it!

Having a growth mindset will help you achieve more regardless of past endeavours or experiences. Our lives are filled with opportunities to shape our path, and next, we will explore the all-important subject of decision-making. By making good decisions, you exercise good leadership so that you can win more as an individual and for the people you help.

"The real voyage of discovery consists not in seeking new landscapes, but in having new eyes."

– Marcel Proust

Chapter 9
Decision-Making
"The Ability to Choose the Best Option"

"He who runs after two rabbits catches none."
– Chinese proverb

The Decision-Making Pillar of Personal Mastery

As we have seen in the previous chapter, having a growth mindset is essential for achieving more and, by nature, opens up opportunities that would not have been expected. When confronted with multiple opportunities, what does one do? Do you jump onto new ones without further thought, or prefer to think through what to do before acting? Do you make use of all promising opportunities? Here, we explore what decision-making is, why it is important and what can be done to improve this for ourselves.

The Chinese proverb about the person who "chases after two rabbits" warns us of the consequences of divided focus – achieving little of real value. The lesson here is the importance of directing our attention and effort toward one goal at a time. This puts an end to the belief that multitasking is a productive way to operate.

Studies show that switching from one task to another comes at a cost. Too much task-switching can interfere with our cognitive capacities, including working memory and long-term memory. It can also impair our ability to do "deep work," which is our best work that requires deep focus and attention. You may have experienced this impairment when you try to work while many distractions are present and vying for your attention.

Decisions are the choices we make. You could say that our lives are the result of all the choices made between the day we were born and the last day we have in this world. In that light, the choices or decisions we make matter. Some will be key, important ones, while others may be small and, when repeatedly done through habit, lead to significant changes over time.

Definitions and Origins of the Word "Decision"

So, what is a decision? The word "decide" comes from the Latin verb *decidere*, which combines "de" (a preposition meaning "away, off, down from") and "caedo, caedere" (a verb meaning "to cut, kill, or slay"). To decide means to cut away what is unnecessary, resulting in a "decision." By cutting away what is unnecessary, you are left with what *is* necessary, allowing you to give it complete focus.

The Chinese word for decision or to decide is "决定" (jué dìng), in which the two characters literally mean "decide" and "set." This suggests the meaning of "making certain" – to make something more certain and known. When you make a decision, you gain clarity and certainty on what you will do next to move forward.

Historically, people have exercised alternative practices to help them make decisions. Some like relying on pure luck, such as a coin toss. Others rely on divination practices like astrology, runes or the *I Ching*, an ancient Chinese text also called the *Book of Changes*. In Ancient Greece, people came to the Oracle of Delphi to seek guidance. Whether or not you believe these methods are reliable, a common element among them is that the enquirer must first enter a meditative and calm state using a ritual or process – something we can universally and objectively agree is good for decision-making.

I myself have doubts about how effective these methods are in developing one's ability to make independent decisions. The idea of letting luck decide, say, with the flip of a coin, removes our involvement in making our own decisions. In other words, by delegating our responsibility to an external process, we become passive bystanders in our own lives, effectively letting someone or something else decide what is best for us.

If you look back at your life so far, you will become aware of some key decision points. For me, this includes my decision to continue university and pursue PhD studies in chemistry, my choice of career early on within the pharmaceutical industry and later, my decision to leave my corporate career to become the coach, mentor and author I am today. I decided to marry my wife and start a family. Some of these decisions were more challenging to make than others, and I am sure you have experienced this as well.

The Importance of Being Decisive

Actively making decisions is about determining how we want to move forward and make better progress. Decisions are often presented metaphorically as a fork in the path ahead. Being at this juncture, it is on us to determine the path we commit to following, a decision that is often difficult to make. The implications of choosing one option over another, both for ourselves and others, can feel overwhelming.

Decisions arise in many situations. For example, you may be thriving in your corporate career but must decide whether to accept a job offer from another company. Perhaps a team member is underperforming against agreed targets, and with pressure to meet year-end goals, you must determine how to address the issue. Or, you may find yourself dissatisfied with how your team leader manages expectations, prompting you to consider your next steps.

Rather than following the "path of least resistance," we would feel better if we proactively decided for ourselves which path to take. A path of least resistance could take the form of making a decision that is no different from the ones you have made before. Alternatively, it could involve delaying the decision to give yourself more time to decide!

Indeed, a good leader is decisive and able to make decisions that are both easy and hard. The decisive leader strategically and tactically assesses the options and chooses, even with incomplete information. It means being courageous and even feeling fear, given the uncertainty of the outcome. It also means being decisive even when the implications are serious and far-reaching. In a challenging situation, failing to make a decision can be even worse than making the wrong one.

Making Decisions is Risky Business

The American general and diplomat Colin Powell once said, "Don't take action if you only have a 10% chance of being right, but don't wait until you have enough facts to be 100% sure, because then it is always too late." One can never be 100% sure before deciding that it is the right one, but wanting to wait for more certainty is a strategic consideration in itself.

How can one determine whether a decision is right or not? Well, it seems this can only be done in hindsight. Even then, the results of a certain decision can be difficult to discern. We do not have the option of turning back time and playing out an alternative decision to compare outcomes; that happens only in science fiction or fantasy movies! Some strategic thinking experts advocate the "rule of 70%." This decision-making strategy points to deciding

Decision-Making

when you have 70% confidence in having made the right decision. Rather than asking what the right decision is, I suggest you ask yourself what the *best* decision is.

Making decisions is an inherently risky business given the potential for unknowns, but it is absolutely necessary for progress. Some of us like to believe we can accurately predict all possible outcomes, much like AI analysing every potential move in a game of chess to defeat even the most skilled players. However, chess operates on a few set rules – life and the challenges we encounter are much more complex!

Making important decisions that include considering vast amounts of data can be overwhelming, yet we humans can also use our intuition to help determine the best option. It is equally important to logically weigh the advantages and disadvantages of a decision as it is to understand how a particular option makes us feel.

A key component is how a decision is made according to our notions of personal values and principles. As values and principles can differ from person to person, how aligned an option is with oneself can vary. Considerations such as integrity, fairness and purpose all have a part to play. One needs to be clear on the key priorities, too.

Consider your decision-making process, especially important ones in life or work. What do you notice? How confident are you in making a decision? Do you ever resort to tactics like flipping a coin?

Why make the decision in the first place? The reason for making the decision is hugely important. That is to say, "having the end in mind" like how Stephen Covey expresses within his book *The Seven Habits of Highly Effective People*.[21] In other words, the decision made aligns with the overall desired strategic outcome. The decision should relate to affecting something that lies within your control.

I am reminded of a noteworthy exchange in *Alice's Adventures in Wonderland* by Lewis Carroll. Alice asks the Cheshire Cat which way to go. "That depends a good deal on where you want to get to," said the cat, to which Alice responded, "I don't much care where." And the cat says, "Then it doesn't much matter which way to go." If you do not know what your overall aim is, then you can't make a meaningful decision on your next step.

Challenges of Decision-Making

Bias and Emotional Influences

One challenge we may face with decision-making is our biases and emotional influences, which are often unconscious. Ideally, we want to be making decisions objectively and rationally, without preconceived perceptions, but this is virtually impossible. Taking time to reflect on the way we make decisions is one way of becoming aware of this, as is working closely with a coach. Our emotional state has an important role to play too. When you are feeling stressed or anxious, your ability to choose the best option is easily impaired. Our decision-making capacity is negatively impacted when we are overwhelmed by the volume of important decisions to be made within a short stretch of time.

Capacity for Making Decisions

The capacity that we have to make big decisions is affected by our levels of energy or willpower. When you are tired and drained of energy, you are not as fit to make decisions as compared to when you are rested. Being able to reduce the number of minor trivial decisions in the day can help you preserve your capacity to make big, important decisions. An example is Barack Obama, who during his US Presidency, wore the same colours of suit, shirt and tie to save up the capacity to decide over matters of the country. He once told *Vanity Fair*, "You'll see I wear only grey or blue suits. I'm trying to pare down my decisions. I don't want to make decisions about what I'm eating or wearing. Because I have too many decisions to make."[22]

Obama firmly believed that the act of making a decision eroded one's ability to make further decisions. This is what psychologists call "decision fatigue." This is an explanation for why shopping for groceries can be draining and judges tend to give harsher rulings later in the day!

Perceived Challenges After the Decision is Made

So far, we have considered decision-making as a proactive and strategic act, yet it is not just an intellectual exercise. The US General Norman Schwarzkopf said, "The truth of the matter is that you always know the right thing to do. The hard part is doing it."

This highlights a key challenge in decision-making when the stakes are high – we tend to focus on the difficulties of following through, even when we know we've made the right choice. Going back to the earlier exploration in this chapter on the origins of the word decision, we can consider cutting away the possibility of turning back and only moving forward. The challenge can feel overwhelming when it is moving into altogether unfamiliar territory. Most decisions we face require us to use a combination of reason and rationality, and intention and feeling to make.

Timeframe

One big factor that affects decision-making is the time available in a given situation. If we give ourselves more time to prepare for a decision, we are more assured that we can choose the best option. Of course, there are times when things are changing so fast and unpredictably that making a decision, much less the best one, can be very challenging.

When there is very little or no time for analysis or reasoning, we may have to do something decisive, relying on intuition or feeling. If you are white water rafting down a raging river, strewn with rocks and sudden drops, you will have to act fast and hope for the best. Furthermore, the timeframe for our decision's effects to manifest will vary. Steering a huge oil tanker at sea is vastly different from steering a small rowboat. The oil tanker is going to require more forward-thinking and action to get the desired result as compared to the small boat. The circumstances for a decision can vary hugely with regard to the duration of time available to prepare and make the decision and for the outcome to be realised.

Decision-Making is an Improvable Skill

Where does this exploration of the huge topic of decision-making leave us? It is an important skill of leadership and strategic behaviour. With this skill, we can become more aware of the decisions we are presented with, along with their significance. We have looked at some common challenges faced when deciding on matters of importance. In my work coaching clients, decision-making is a frequently encountered theme. Roadblocks include the avoidance of decision-making or overthinking (e.g. "analysis paralysis"), a diminished capacity to make good decisions due to stress and being overwhelmed and the lack of clarity on personal aims and values.

Like the other pillars covered in this book, decision-making skills can be improved through better self awareness, self management and self confidence. Again, like other disciplines and skills, becoming more proficient at decision-making necessitates more experience in making decisions in the real world.

The most effective way to improve your decision-making skills is to make more of them. No amount of thinking and learning can substitute for the practical experience gained from doing. Here is my framework, the "6 C's of Decision Making," to help you develop your ability to make important choices.

The 6 C's of Decision Making

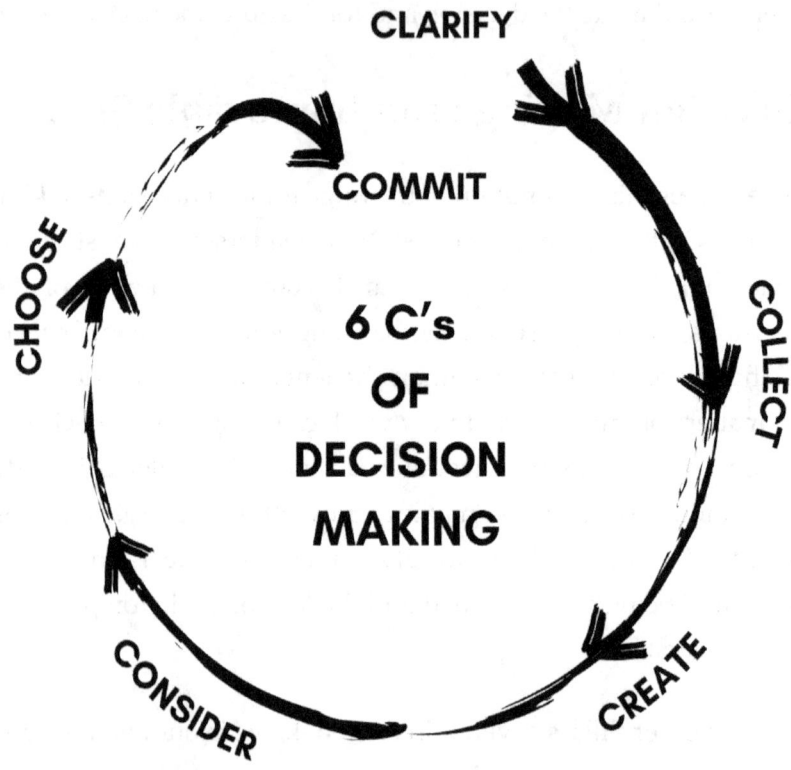

Clarify. Clarify the decision to be made and its context. Clarify the context of this decision among others you have in front of you. If you have many decisions to make, use the Eisenhower matrix (see Resources section) by organising each decision into one of four quadrants: Urgent/Important, Non-Urgent/Important, Urgent/Non-Important, and Non-Urgent/Non-Important.

Get clear on what this decision helps you achieve and what a good decision will look like to you. Get clarity on the timeframe of the decision to be made and for outcomes to be observed.

Collect. Collect key data you need to make an informed decision.

Create. Create several options. Do not think about what is possible or not at this stage.

Consider. Consider each option you created in the previous step in terms of practicalities, benefits and risks, perspectives and possible biases. Seek counsel from others as needed.

Choose. Choose the most viable option.

Commit. Commit to your chosen option!

You have made your decision. Now communicate and act on it!

There will be situations where you may not have the luxury of time to carefully consider and choose. In these situations, quick decisions will need to be made with known and unknown uncertainties. You will just become more experienced at making these quick decisions and learn from them! For additional material to help you here, refer to the Resources section of this book.

Winning More

Summary

"Winning More," as we have explored in this section, covers mindsets that we can develop to help us keep growing and achieve more.

Making decisions effectively is a huge factor in life. Things change as we do, and decisions enable us to determine how we progress. Indeed, decision-making is a key skill of leadership, an ability to determine for ourselves how we want to move forward. Getting better at making decisions no matter how weighty they may be involves getting more deliberate practice. In the Resources section of this book, you can get access to exclusive online resources to help you develop your decision-making skills. Seeking help from a coach or mentor can be a great support.

I hope you take full ownership of your decisions, empowering yourself to make the most of both your work and personal life. Decisions made at work can impact your life outside of it, and the reverse can be very true too. So it is important to choose wisely!

Decisions vary, but what truly matters is the goal they lead to and, to some extent, their significance and meaning. In the next chapter, we'll explore these nuances further under the theme of purpose.

> *"Your life changes the moment you make a new, congruent and committed decision."*
>
> – Tony Robbins

Section 4
Finding Purpose

"The meaning of life is to find your gift. The purpose of life is to give it away."

– Pablo Picasso

Chapter 10
Purpose
"Having a Sense of Meaning and Direction in One's Life"

"The two most important days in your life are the day you are born and the day you find out why."
– Mark Twain

Finding Purpose

The Purpose Pillar of Personal Mastery

What brings you here?

Isn't that an interesting question? You are likely to have read the previous chapters of this book from the first to this one, the tenth – and I'd say the most important one. We covered Personal Mastery topics that help you take back control of your life and work, then start leading and onwards to win more! Here, we come to the point where we ask why this journey in personal development matters: It is about finding purpose.

The previous chapter covered decision-making. You have reached this point in your life having made it through countless decision points, some more notable than others, some you made the choice and others someone else or circumstances determined things for you. So whether you've decided every step you made to get to this point or not, the truth is that you are here, right now. So what now?

In fact, those three words, "So what now?" were what struck me in my own writing journey for this very book! My interpretation, if you will, is to be revealed in the next pages. All the earlier chapter topics lead here.

Our Fascination With Why

I define the concept of purpose as having a sense of meaning and direction in our lives. The simple question "Why?" is incredibly powerful. It's my favourite among the question words – alongside what, how, when, who, and which. This question also happens to be the most difficult one to answer.

Young children are inquisitive and constantly open to learning about the world that they live in. Beyond observing what things are and what they do, asking the why question attributes meaning and reasoning. If you have ever taken care of a child, you have likely been bombarded by "Why?" After several attempts at giving satisfactory answers, I can't blame you if you've resorted to the very unsatisfactory parental motto of, "Because I said so!"

I am curious about the reasons people do things or the rationale for doing things in a certain way. I recall once arriving late at a company training workshop about change management. When I entered, they were discussing a hypothetical scenario of a planned major office relocation project. The delegates were in the middle of calling out questions on what they wanted to know the answers to. Jumping in cold without preamble, I asked, "Why is this office move taking place?" No one else had asked the why question, yet there was no shortage of questions on what, how, when, who, which – in short, all relating to what the project was, but nothing previously on the rationale for the big change! The trainer remarked on how I asked the most insightful question after having just "parachuted" into the situation. I later thought about why this was.

We tend to focus on understanding what is happening because it feels more immediate and easier to answer, while the deeper insight of why is often overlooked – at least at the moment. Is the "why?" a more strategic question compared to what, how, who, where and when?

The Five Whys

What we observe as an event is actually the effect of an underlying cause. There is a cause-and-effect relationship that we envisage being present. Asking "why?" gives an insight into the cause for an effect, and asking this repeatedly allows us to explore more deeply what they are.

There is a technique called the "Five Whys," described by Taiichi Ohno of the Toyota Motor Corporation, which we can use to diagnose the cause-and-effect relationship underlying a specific problem.[23] By asking "why?" five times, we can better identify the root causes of a defect or problem. There is no guarantee here that asking five times is sufficient or indeed more than sufficient, but it speaks of the intention to understand the reason for an event taking place. It can also be applied to identifying the underlying motivation for doing something.

Films, TV shows and novels encourage us to seek the underlying causes of events. The most popular titles are crime dramas and "whodunit" stories. I myself was a huge fan of the *Lost* series from the 2000s, which had a lot of its viewers asking "why?" way too many times. The story circles a group of plane crash survivors stuck on a mysterious island somewhere in the South Pacific Ocean. Amid supernatural events, viewers were given flashback sequences that helped make sense of the survivors' individual lives before they got aboard the ill-fated plane.

As the TV series proceeded, we got answers to the "how" behind them getting on the plane and what they did; the "what" that brought them there – their objective; and the "why" they were there – their reason for what they wanted to achieve.

To me, the constant compelling theme and basis for great storytelling throughout the series was "why?" A great story will

Finding Purpose

always have a great "why." I could go further to say that a great story will always have a great lesson to take from it.

Lost was a TV series that was a work of fiction, intended to entertain. Imagine how much more compelling a story might be when it is a true one!

Hero of Purpose: Dashrath Manjhi (1934-2007)

One such story concerns a man named Dashrath Manjhi in India.[24] I'll summarise his story using how, what and why here as follows:

How: Manjhi used simple tools – a hammer and chisel – and worked for 22 years to carve a path through a mountain, often alone and against great odds. He also faced ridicule from other people.

What: He created a 110-metre-long road, 7.7 metres deep in places and 9.1 metres wide through a ridge of rock.

Why: His goal was to spare others from the suffering his wife endured when she tragically passed away due to delayed medical care caused by the mountain barrier. He sought to improve access and transform his community's lives.

This man's feat, which took 22 years from 1960 to 1982, is nothing short of miraculous. He did it with a hammer, chisel and his own manpower alone! He carved a path through so much solid rock! Through it all, it was his motivation, his drive, his purpose and his why that kept him going. The path he made reduced the distance between his home of Atri and the Waziganj section of the Gaya district from 55 km to 15 km. Ultimately, he created something he wished had existed when his wife was in urgent need of prompt medical attention. Instead of letting the tragedy paralyse him, he decided that he was going to use his grief to fuel this awe-inspiring act.

At first, his fellow villagers mocked Manjhi, but later on, they began lending support by giving him food and helping him buy tools. The fact that this man left a lasting legacy and lived with purpose and meaning is truly inspiring, even though his journey was born from tragedy.

If you were one of the villagers watching Manjhi tirelessly working on the mountain ridge, it would be understandable to see his task as futile – it had never been done before. Yet, knowing his purpose, you might feel compelled to help, even as a gesture of solidarity with him and his cause.

In this amazing story, Manjhi had a compelling purpose, a why. It enabled him to keep going to overcome a seemingly impossible task.

People may like how you do things and what you do, but they are less likely to forget *why* you do it! This reminds me of a famous saying from the great mind of Maya Angelou: "I've learned that people will forget what you said, people will forget what you did, but people will never forget how you made them feel." As Friedrich Nietzsche observed, "He who has a why to live can bear almost any how."

Finding Purpose

Manjhi literally did the next best thing to moving a mountain. He cut a path through it. He more than earned the nickname "Mountain Man"!

Starting From Why

When I recounted the inspiring story of Manjhi, I introduced the facts in the order of "how" he did what he did, then "what" he set out to achieve, and lastly, "why" he set out to achieve it. This can be summarised as follows:

How: Used a hammer and chisel to carve a path through a mountain, which took 22 years.

What: A path through a mountain.

Why: To prevent others from suffering as his wife did and to transform the lives of his community.

But if we look at this the other way, we get:

Why: To prevent others from suffering as his wife did and to transform the lives of his community.

What: A path through a mountain.

How: Used a hammer and chisel to carve a path through a mountain, which took 22 years.

It makes better sense to us when we view the story of Manjhi from the perspective of why. The lesson here is that it is easier to connect with people when we know their why. While it does not need to arise from a personal calamity as in Manjhi's case, that why can also be to serve or fulfil a purpose that is more than themselves, a cause that helps others. By having a why behind what we do, we establish meaning and direction for our lives. Our why determines what we choose to do, and the way that we do it, the how.

This why does not need to be universally true for everyone, but it does need to be true for you. It needs to be personally relevant. It needs to be owned by you alone.

Philosophical Perspectives on Why

In the whole history of human civilisation, we humans have sought to understand the universe we live in. When our early ancestors looked up at the sun, they were aware that it moved through the sky and disappeared from view at night, only to reappear the next day. They noticed how this affected animals and plants. Recognising these patterns was useful for survival, safety and meeting other needs. But there remains the bigger underlying question: "Why?" To our knowledge to date, we appear to be the only creatures that need to know why. Why seems to be central to human experience. Let's explore what we humans have recognised from a philosophical point of view.

Existentialism: The Search for Meaning

Asking why is key to our deepest questions: Why do I exist? Why does anything matter?

Many people have considered what meaning is attached to our existence. One notable thinker was Viktor Frankl. He put forward the idea that meaning is the main driver of human life, even amidst suffering. His observations were captured in his book *Man's Search For Meaning,* which tells his experiences as a Jewish prisoner in Auschwitz during the Second World War.[25] He saw that there were fellow prisoners who had a why to live for and others who did not. Frankl later developed a form of therapy called logotherapy, derived from the Greek word for meaning, *"logos."* This therapy helps patients focus on the meaning of human existence as well as the search for such a meaning.

Epistemology: The Basis of Inquiry

Just like the young children described earlier in this chapter who like to ask "Why?", the question "Why?" is central to the aim of philosophy – to seek knowledge and understanding. Philosophers like Aristotle considered "Why?" to be key to discovering the causes behind events, leading from superficial observation to deeper comprehension. Asking "Why?" allows us to get to an understanding of the essence and purpose of things.

Teleology: The Pursuit of Purpose

The act of asking "Why?" can help us examine whether there is an inherent purpose in the universe or our lives. Teleology is the branch of philosophy that looks at the purpose or end goal of things. The term is derived from the ancient Greek word *"telos,"* meaning "end, purpose, goal." The similar Greek word "teleō" is spoken in the Bible in John 19:30, meaning "it is finished." The word "autotelic" is applied to describe an activity or creative work that has an end or purpose in itself.

We have differing views on whether the universe and the world we live in or our lives have a purpose. These can give rise to the voicing of perspectives like Theism, which argues that life has a divine or cosmological purpose or Atheism, which argues that meaning is constructed by the individual rather than given inherently.

The way we perceive our own "why" shapes how we interpret our place in the world.

Morals and Ethics

When we ask the question "why?", we challenge ourselves to examine our values and actions. Asking "why?" to determine ethical behaviour was explored by philosophers like Immanuel Kant and John Stuart Mill. Kant looked at the "why" of morality as being grounded in reason and universal principles. Mill looked at the "why" of morality as relating to the greatest happiness or utility. By asking "why?", we face the motivations behind our actions, promoting our moral growth and responsibility.

Our Unique Capacity to Wonder and Question

Humans, as far as we are aware, are unique in that we have the capacity to wonder about our world and question to understand it. By asking "why" in the context, we raise our awareness of our being and its context in the mystery and awe of existence. This drives us to progress, create and grow our potential.

From a philosophical perspective, the use of "why?" challenges assumptions and conventions. It is key to critical examination and thinking. Thinkers like Socrates were champions of asking this to strip away layers of unexamined beliefs. The "why?" question frees us from dogma and promotes intellectual freedom, exploration and expression.

Having gone through this cursory overview of the philosophical perspective of "why", we see how central this question has been to us since ancient times and remains just as relevant today. It is a key component of human inquiry and existence. It is a central theme that keeps us in the pursuit of understanding and serves as a reference point for us to lead a meaningful and examined life.

From this exploration, you are now at a point of better awareness of this and likely want to go further. My belief and understanding are that everyone has a why, even if people may not be fully aware of it.

What Happens When We Become Detached From Our Why?

Let us explore this first through a couple of fictional narrative examples.

The Lotus Eaters from *The Odyssey*

In Greek mythology's epic story of the travels of Odysseus, the protagonist and his ship crew encounter a race of people called "Lotus Eaters." The island these people were living on was notable for the dominant presence of the lotus tree, whose fruits were their main food. Unfortunately, the lotus fruit had narcotic properties that left those who ate it in a peaceful yet apathetic sleep. Those who consumed it forgot their home and loved ones and only cared about staying on the island to continue eating the fruit. They no longer felt responsibility.

From this story, the term "lotus eater" describes people who spend their time indulging in pursuits of pleasure and luxury instead of handling practical concerns. While we are inclined to pursue pleasure, it can feel unnatural to live for pleasure without regard to the people and concerns that we care about. When we become distanced from our why, we risk living aimlessly and ruining our better selves.

What observations on your own life and work are prompted by this story of the lotus eaters?

Neo in *The Matrix*

Early on in *The Matrix*, Neo leads a life without personal fulfilment. He works a mundane corporate job as a programmer and goes by the generic name "Mr. Anderson." His life is unremarkable. The office where he works is impersonal and sterile, made of identical cubicles. His superiors are demanding, often chastising him for being late and not conforming. He feels isolated, with no meaningful relationships, connection or joy. He has a nagging feeling that something is missing from his life but is unable to identify it.

The character Neo feels trapped, empty and lost. His life is routine and not aligned with a meaningful why. It highlights the need to find it for himself. This tells us that we have a need for a why. This can spur us to look for it. This involves becoming more connected with it through a better understanding of what it is.

What observations on your own life and work are prompted by this story of Neo?

Heroes of Purpose Who Found Their Why

Next, let us explore how some real people who did not know their "why" later found it:

Mahatma Gandhi

When Mahatma Gandhi was a young adult, he was very shy and introverted. While a law student in England, he struggled to fit in socially. His studies in law were not prompted by passion, but for reasons of it being considered a respectable profession and encouraged by his family. After the completion of his studies, Gandhi struggled to establish a legal career in India. It was not helped by his inability to speak confidently in court. He felt directionless and unsure of how to contribute meaningfully to society.

Gandhi later moved to South Africa to work as a legal advisor. He faced racial discrimination, including being thrown off a train for his racial identity. These experiences affected him deeply, to the extent that he began to see himself as part of the collective struggle against injustice. He gained the personal conviction that this fight for civil rights was where his purpose lay. This was the fight he became well known for, always with non-violence and vision. He became the leader of India's independence movement.

Lee Kuan Yew

Lee Kuan Yew was born to a middle-class Chinese family in British-ruled Singapore. On one hand, he experienced privilege, and on the other, the limitations of being part of a colonised society. He excelled in law studies while at university in England, but he had great difficulty reconciling the Western ideas he encountered with the reality of colonial oppression back home in Singapore. His legal career in Singapore left him feeling unfulfilled. At the time post World War II, he saw firsthand the vulnerability of his people amid poverty, racial tension and weak governance. From this environment, Lee made a bold step to co-found the People's Action Party (PAP) in 1954, and he committed to Singapore's independence and secure future.

The examples of Gandhi and Lee show people who did not know their why at first but later found it for themselves. As they went through life, they developed and discovered themselves, becoming aware of the difference that they could make. Your childhood dreams of what you wanted to become are likely very different from who you are now.

What were your childhood dreams? How different are they from the life that you have now?

Reflecting on my own journey, my why has certainly changed from my youth. I had dreams of becoming a doctor to heal people and have the recognition and prestige that this career brought. My why changed to helping ensure that people in need of medicines, especially in the developing world, had access to them. My love of learning and self development led me to share what I learned and help others. This became my why: helping others fulfil their potential.

My why has changed over time, but the difference now compared to my younger days is in how intimately I connected with it. The more I connected with my why, the more I was driven by it. Having a close connection to my why is a reliable source of self motivation and self confidence. It gives me a sense of conviction in how I choose to live my life now. It is my close connection with my why that led me to leave the corporate ladder, become a professional coach and literally put pen to paper to write this very book for you, my reader!

Your Own Journey to Finding Purpose

Reading and hearing about other people who have a sense of purpose in life is one thing. But what about you? What connection do you have with your purpose or why?

How does the work you do feel to you? Where is your career taking you if you keep going in the direction you see? What areas do you see yourself growing in? What do you want your life to mean? What do you want to do differently and for what reason?

Answering these questions can feel very daunting. They are not easy questions that come with quick answers. How you answer them depends on your own perspective, your own experiences and your current way of life and work.

The key to exploring these types of questions is to take note of your observations, reflections and learnings as you find them. Writing down questions you have is also part of the explorative process. You could write down these notes in a journal so that you can build on what you have discovered before. I like to tell my clients to avoid aiming for better answers and instead discover better questions to explore. That is a growth mindset attribute that I can offer to you on this journey of self exploration.

If you feel you need a stronger sense of meaning or direction in your life, then you are in the right place. I will walk you through some simple steps to improve your chances of being successful.

If you feel that you already have a good sense of meaning or direction in your life, you may find what I am going to share to be helpful to you for improving clarity on your current thinking.

Using My A.L.I.G.N. Framework to Find Your Why

The exploration of what constitutes purpose and meaning is a journey of self discovery. It is an innately personal one. If one sets out with the intention of discovering it, that is certainly a great start. However, just like the idea of setting out on a journey into the great unknown without a sense of direction or clear objectives, you can easily become lost. For this reason, having clear objectives and a structure is going to be key for a purposeful journey of self discovery. Below is my A.L.I.G.N. framework that will give you the required structure and clarity:

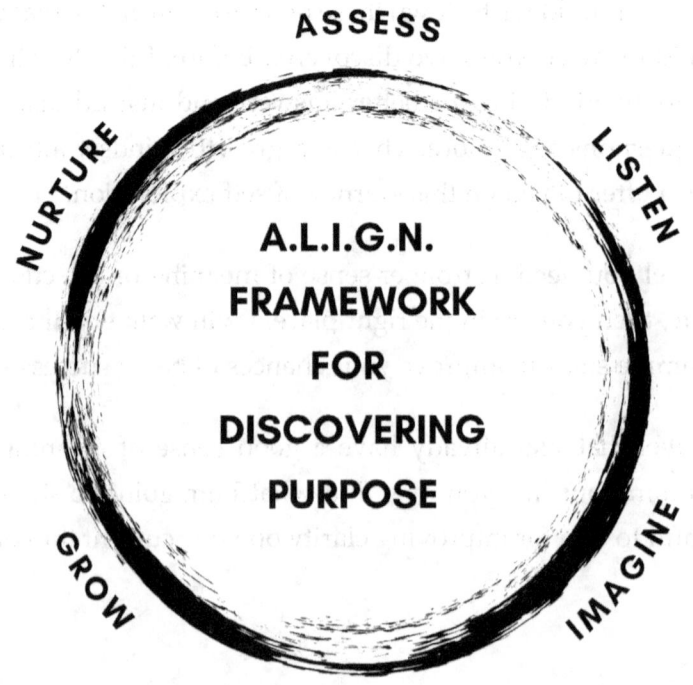

Assess

It is important to evaluate your current starting point.

Take a look at what is working well for you in life and work, as well as what is not working well. Write down recent notable events, positive or negative, from which you felt a distinctive way or learned important lessons. Do not forget that you can draw on other people you trust to give informed and constructive feedback too.

Ask yourself these questions: What brings me joy and energy? What drains me of energy or makes me feel out of place?

Some situations can make you light up and feel energised. Conversely, there may be times when you feel the loss of your own vitality or you feel you don't fit in.

Make an inventory of your values, strengths and passions:

Values. Create a table of three equal columns. Jot down your values into the lefthand column. These are core principles that you strive to live by. If you were to describe your character or the way you conduct yourself, what words would you use?

Strengths. In the middle column, write down your greatest strengths. These can include your interpersonal capabilities as well as your defined technical strengths. You may have had a friend, colleague or peer remark about your noticeable strengths.

Passions. Lastly, write down in the rightmost column the things you are most passionate about. This can include causes that you feel strongly about or hobbies and interests you like to spend time on.

Listen

Now, we go deeper. We tune into what some call the inner voice.

Study your inner voice. When you have a moment to yourself in a calm and peaceful setting, what thoughts and feelings come to you? What do they say about what you are aware of? What do they say about what you consider to be meaningful?

Explore past experiences. Looking back on your life and work, what pivotal experiences have you had that you find particularly meaningful? These can be moments when you become more aware of something important to you.

Pose these questions to yourself and see what answers and thoughts come up: When have I felt most alive? If I were fearless, what would I do?

Imagine

Find a quiet moment to do this visualisation with your eyes closed. Visualise an ideal life or career aligned with purpose and meaning for you. What would the people around you be like? How would you be feeling? Ask yourself these questions: If I were living fully in alignment with what I find meaningful, what would my days look like and feel like? What impact would I be making?

If you think that you currently have no clarity yet on what your ideal life or career is, then you can explore the possibilities while keeping an open mind. This is an invaluable experience as you are actively exploring what is currently unknown to you so that more clarity ensues. This exercise can work better for you when you have someone to guide you through it. Make a note of the discoveries you make.

Grow

Review what you have discovered in the earlier steps of the A.L.I.G.N. framework, then identify small, actionable steps to take you closer to your envisioned future. As you make committed small steps forward, you will start getting more clarity on the type of future you find meaningful.

Create opportunities to understand more and test what is meaningful and valuable to you. These are effectively like mini-experiments set up for yourself. They can include volunteering, classes, travel, workshops, new roles at work etc.

Committing to ongoing growth and adaptability is important, especially as you are looking for meaningful change. That would mean a significant change from previous personal notions of life and work. Working with a coach here can really help!

Nurture

The search for meaning and purpose is not a quick and easy endeavour. It takes time, sustained effort and progress. It is unlikely to follow a simple straight line! Applying practices to remain resilient over the long run will help in the discovery journey and beyond. Regularly review progress and check that it still aligns with your goals and values.

Develop the self discoveries you made doing this exercise by doing it again. This reiteration is part of the Nurture step to keep refining and exploring what is meaningful and purposeful to you.

One of the merits of my A.L.I.G.N. framework is that it gives structure and simplicity to the self discovery journey needed to explore what is considered to be purposeful and meaningful. The framework breaks down the seemingly insurmountable task into more manageable steps while maintaining the renewal of efforts aligned with the overall aim. For additional resources to help you apply the A.L.I.G.N. framework, refer to the Resources section of this book.

The value of my A.L.I.G.N. framework to you would be elevated even more when you work with a coach, thereby freeing yourself of knowing in detail the steps and process involved. Working closely with a coach can significantly improve the timeframe for you to discover what your purpose could be and create more meaning for you in work and life.

Purpose

I like to use my A.L.I.G.N. framework when I work with my clients who want to be more connected to their why, have a sense of purpose in what they do and have more meaning in life and work. I also apply my A.L.I.G.N. framework to strengthen my sense of my own why. I hope that you'll find yours too!

Summary

The "Why?" question is intriguing and key to our own experience of life and work. By becoming more connected and familiar with our own why, we can do our best work and have the greatest impact on the lives of others as well as our own.

In this chapter of the "Finding Purpose" section, we explored the appeal of the why question, even from a philosophical perspective. We find that we are also attracted to others when we see them articulating clearly their why and acting in alignment with it. Finding out our own why is an endeavour that takes time spent in self discovery, and the rewards will become apparent when that why is fully embraced. With a stronger connection to your purpose, you will have a source of motivation to keep you moving forward and achieving and winning! You will have the strongest reason available to you on why you do what you choose to do. I have shared my simple A.L.I.G.N. framework to help you discover your why so that you can take full ownership of it and go fully into it! Finding purpose is an endeavour that is ingrained in the essence of being fully human.

> *"The purpose of life is not to be happy. It is to be useful, to be honourable, to be compassionate, to have it make some difference that you have lived and lived well."*
>
> – Ralph Waldo Emerson

Conclusion

In this book, we explored the 10 pillars of my Personal Mastery Method framework to help you become a better leader of yourself. With this newfound insight, you may find yourself asking more questions about yourself to live and work to your fullest potential. This is a positive step, as living fully isn't about having all the answers – it's about continuously seeking deeper understanding.

Jung Personal Mastery Method

As is good practice after completing such an important journey, let us revisit some of the key areas covered.

Take Back Control

Self Awareness

If you realise that the life that you have just happens to you rather than with you directing it, you need to exert more control. You can only direct what is within your control and realising this is of vital importance. Furthermore, you will need to understand what you can control and have a reliable means to observe the way you are doing things, the words you say and your feelings and thoughts. Taking back control starts from looking within via the application of self awareness. By monitoring your thoughts, feelings, words and actions, you will get a reliable read on how you are performing and how much you are making in terms of progress and improvements.

Self Knowledge

Next, you study yourself and get to know and understand yourself, your strengths, weaknesses, preferences and unique experiences. You will get a comprehensive overview of your capabilities, interests and passions.

Self Management

With the foundation of self awareness and self knowledge, you can implement better self management for yourself so that you can perform at your best every day. You will feel better too as you practise better self care.

Starting to Lead

An ability to take control of what is within your control is effectively the ability to lead. This leadership capability means that you become more fully functional, being able to meet important needs with awareness, knowledge and application. You will have an improved level of impact on your life and work.

Self Motivation

Leading requires you to initiate sustained change. It requires you to understand what behaviours and inner thoughts drive you towards success and achievement versus what does not. It asks of you to be clear on the utmost importance of the reason for the envisaged change. This is coupled with a strong desire for the intended outcome.

Resilience

It has been said that the way to success is often paved with failure. The environment changes. We are required to be tough, to withstand the falls failure gives us, and to have the flexibility to adapt to ever-present change. Our trained ability to keep getting back up and moving forward results in greater chances of overall success and achievement.

Self Confidence

Working towards success and achievement involves facing fears of the unknown, including our own capabilities. By trusting in ourselves and our abilities, and accepting that fear is a natural part of the human experience of doing new untried acts, we can do what we previously would not have imagined for ourselves.

Winning More

Self confidence, the drive to progress, and the ability to handle challenges amid change are foundational for leadership in life and work. For greater impact as leaders, we need to further enhance our mindsets, which enable us to look for possibilities, develop them into opportunities, and make our choices on how to move forward.

Realistic Optimism

By choosing to act on what is within your control, you can navigate through whatever change is happening around you. This brings into play the realisation that each one of us has the freedom to act through choice. It involves adopting the mindset of viewing situations in a positive light, even difficult ones, as opportunities for taking intentional action.

Growth Mindset

The growth mindset enables us to keep learning, growing and evolving. It allows us to question how things can be done more effectively, what can be learned, and what can be applied to situations encountered and to ourselves. This helps us focus on solutions to challenges as a way forward rather than remaining rooted in the problem.

Decision Making

The ability to be decisive is a key trait of strong leadership. This ability is all the more critical in situations that are uncertain, complex and constantly evolving, with the absence of complete data to hand. It involves full trust in deciding the optimal course of action and handling and facing the resulting outcomes, be they desired or not, expected or unexpected. It requires clarity in the intended objective.

Finding Purpose

A leader who is acquainted with good self awareness, has knowledge of themselves, exercises self care reliably, has good drive, resilience and self confidence, has an empowering mindset and can be decisive is a good leader. But all these qualities would have little lasting impact if the leader had no connection with their bigger why, their sense of purpose and life direction. They would be leading as an incomplete individual, not being able to live in a fulfilled, meaningful way. The leader who is closely connected to their purpose is not only empowered fully but has the impact to lead others to fulfil their potential to become their best selves.

Here is an overview of the 10 pillars of personal mastery:

Taking Back Control	*Self Awareness*	Observing your own thoughts, feelings, words and actions leads to being able to understand how you operate.
	Self Knowledge	A deep understanding of yourself means you know your unique experience and abilities. You realise what you are capable of. You become more able to direct what you understand about yourself.
	Self Management	Understanding and meeting your own needs (physical, emotional, mental, spiritual).

Conclusion

Starting To Lead	*Self Motivation*	All lasting personal change for personal improvement needs a sustained drive to effect.
	Resilience	Successful progress is made by embracing failures along the way. What matters is getting back up after each fall, moving forward and adapting to change.
	Self Confidence	It is fine to feel fear when you face the unknown or new challenges. By trusting in yourself, you can move forward with your efforts while still feeling fear.
Winning More	*Realistic Optimism*	Realising you have the freedom to take meaningful action on what is within your control can help you achieve and grow.
	Growth Mindset	You can choose a more empowering mindset for yourself, one that sees opportunity in success and failure alike, so you can keep learning and growing in your abilities.
	Decision Making	You can take ownership of your own choices to lead yourselves and others.
Finding Purpose	*Purpose*	You need to be connected to your "why" and have a sense of your direction in life. This enables you to live in a fulfilling way and become fully yourself.

We have uncovered the 10 pillars – the whats – that make up what I call Personal Mastery, the practice of becoming our best selves and leading in life and work. I have shared some "hows" and strategies to help you develop in each of those pillars. But what about the "why" behind personal mastery?

I believe that anyone who truly cares can take full ownership of themselves. Does personal mastery guarantee success and fulfillment? I say it is a guaranteed start to moving in that direction, and it all depends on how fully you take personal ownership of it.

With this book, my hope and wish is that you take up that ownership so that you can attain more personal mastery for yourself, your loved ones, your peers and neighbours, and the world. What a wonderful life of purpose, with meaning and direction, that would be.

Go forth and flex those wings!

> *"The privilege of a lifetime is to become who you truly are."*
>
> – Carl Jung

Epilogue

Do you realise you don't have to do this alone? Your chances of success are much higher with dedicated support. Having the right guidance allows you to integrate personal mastery into your life efficiently, without wasting valuable time and effort.

If you want to explore this further, then visit the link or scan the QR code below:

https://jungpersonalmastery.com/pm-book-resources/

Resources

For bonus resources to help you get more value out of this book, use the link or scan the QR code below:

https://jungpersonalmastery.com/pm-book-resources/

References

[1] Goleman, D. *Emotional Intelligence*. London: Bloomsbury, 1996.

[2] Frankl, V. *Man's Search for Meaning*. London: Rider, 2004.

[3] Lao Tzu. *Tao Te Ching*. London: Penguin Classics, 2008.

[4] The Myers & Briggs Foundation. 'MBTI Basics'. Available at: https://www.myersbriggs.org (accessed 7 March 2025).

[5] —. 'MBTI Basics'. Available at: https://www.myersbriggs.org (accessed 7 March 2025).

[6] Maslow, A. H. 'A Theory of Human Motivation'. *Psychological Review*, 50 (1943), pp. 370–396.

[7] Koltko-Rivera, M. E. 'Self-Transcendence: Maslow's Answer to Cultural Closeness'. *Review of General Psychology*, 10 (2006), pp. 302–317.

[8] Huffington, A. *Thrive*. London: WH Allen, 2014.

⁹ Covey, S. R. *First Things First*. New York: Free Press, 1994.

¹⁰ Nestor, J. Breath: *The New Science of a Lost Art*. London: Penguin Life, 2020.

¹¹ Amen, D. *Change Your Brain, Change Your Life*. New York: Harmony Books, 1998.

¹² Clear, J. *Atomic Habits*. London: Random House Business, 2018.

¹³ World Health Organization. 'Burn-out an Occupational Phenomenon: International Classification of Diseases'. 28 May 2019. Available at: https://www.who.int/news/item/28-05-2019-burn-out-an-occupational-phenomenon-international-classification-of-diseases (accessed 7 March 2025).

¹⁴ 'Stanford Marshmallow Experiment'. *Wikipedia*. Available at: https://en.wikipedia.org/wiki/Stanford_marshmallow_experiment (accessed 7 March 2025).

¹⁵ Mandela, N. *Long Walk to Freedom*. London: Little, Brown, 1994.

¹⁶ Clance, P. R. & Imes, S. A. 'The Imposter Phenomenon in High Achieving Women: Dynamics and Therapeutic Intervention'. *Psychotherapy: Theory, Research & Practice*, **15** (1978), pp. 241–247.

¹⁷ Amen Clinics. 'The Number One Habit to Develop in Order to Feel More Positive'. Available at: https://www.amenclinics.com/blog/number-one-habit-develop-order-feel-positive (accessed 7 March 2025).

[18] Kwik, J. 'Kwik Brain 030: End Negative Self-Talk Like Magic'. Available at: https://www.jimkwik.com/podcasts/kwik-brain-030-end-negative-self-talk-like-magic/ (accessed 7 March 2025).

[19] Schneider, S. L. 'In Search of Realistic Optimism: Meaning, Knowledge, and Warm Fuzziness'. *American Psychologist*, **56** (2001), pp. 250–263.

[20] Dweck, C. Mindset: *The New Psychology of Success*. New York: Random House, 2006.

[21] Covey, S. R. *The Seven Habits of Highly Effective People*. New York: Free Press, 1989.

[22] The Guardian. 'Barack Obama's Secret Weapon: His Steady Routine'. 17 September 2012. Available at: https://www.theguardian.com/world/shortcuts/2012/sep/17/barack-obama-secret-weapon-routine (accessed 7 March 2025).

[23] Ohno, T. *Toyota Production System: Beyond Large-Scale Production*. New York: Productivity Press, 1988.

[24] 'Dashrath Manjhi'. *Wikipedia*. Available at: https://en.wikipedia.org/wiki/Dashrath_Manjhi (accessed 7 March 2025).

[25] —. *Man's Search for Meaning*. London: Rider, 2004.

Acknowledgements

Writing a book is not as easy as typing up a few thoughts or putting pen to paper. The writing experience is so much more than that. Doubts and questions lie in wait to hinder the intrepid author's progress. The result of this book is a testament to the team of supporters who have helped me on my writing journey and made it feel less like a lonely pursuit!

My heartfelt thanks go to these amazing people:

Chloë Bisson and her team at Inspired By Publishing for their guidance and support. I want to especially thank my writing coach Angela Haynes-Ranger for her diligent and ever-reliable support on my writing journey.

My graphics designer, Addan Fatima, for her excellent work in creating the diagrams and logos.

My business coach, Tomas Svitorka, whom I approached for support on my initial steps into entrepreneurship, and who graciously accepted the task of writing the foreword.

To my mentors and coaches who have imparted insight and wisdom along the way.

To friends and peers who have eagerly anticipated this book and offered me encouragement when I needed it.

My wonderful children, Daniel and Emily, for their love and support and for being the first to read my initial drafts of the final chapter of this book.

My wife, Yen Ming, for her unwavering support as my life partner and friend. She always believes in me and encourages me to do my best in what I am passionate about.

Last but not least, to God, for giving me this opportunity to fully be myself!

About the Author

Jung Wing Wan, PhD, is a coach, speaker, author and founder of Jung Personal Mastery Ltd., a company based in the UK that specialises in coaching leaders worldwide to perform as the best versions of themselves.

He developed the Jung Personal Mastery Method as a framework for the coaching he provides for clients. This framework was created from his passion for what he calls "personal mastery"– the leading of oneself to perform with presence, excellence and a sense of purpose. He brings into it not only the leadership practices gained from his former corporate career but also from his practice of martial arts and his interest in philosophy.

Before becoming a coach, Jung led a 25-year career within the pharmaceutical industry. During this time, he travelled to over 30 countries to meet with national health authorities or overseas colleagues. He worked on projects that supported research and development, licensing and the availability of essential medicines worldwide.

It was during his pharmaceutical career that he encountered personal challenges with communication and sought to speak with more confidence. He observed how other people spoke – those who did so well and those who did not. He learned a lot from experiencing both success and failure along the way. He learned that being an effective communicator involved not just technique but also the right mindset. Years later, Jung sought speaker coaching from the globally renowned speaker, transformational coach and bestselling author Lisa Nichols.

His early academic path included a PhD in Chemistry and a year in France as an exchange student. He loves learning languages and speaks Chinese (Cantonese and Mandarin), French, and Spanish. He has been married for almost 25 years to Yen Ming, with whom he has two wonderful children, Daniel and Emily. He practises the Chinese martial arts of Tai Chi Chuan (Taiji Quan) and Xing Yi Quan, which have helped him develop his appreciation of the practice of personal mastery. He is an avid callisthenics athlete and runner and loves the art of Chinese cooking and BBQs. He also serves as chairman and elder at a church in central London.